# WANTED MAN

# WANTED MAN

## In Search of Bob Dylan

### Edited by John Bauldie

Citadel Press
Carol Publishing Group
New York

CITADEL UNDERGROUND

First Citadel Underground Edition 1991

Copyright © 1990 by John Bauldie

A Citadel Press Book
Published by Carol Publishing Group
Citadel Press is a registered trademark of Carol Communications, Inc.

Editorial Offices          Sales & Distribution Offices
600 Madison Avenue    120 Enterprise Avenue
New York, NY 10022    Secaucus, NJ 07094

In Canada: Musson Book Company
A division of General Publishing Co. Limited
Don Mills, Ontario M3B 2T6

First published by Black Spring Press, London, 1990

Manufactured in the United States of America
10  9  8  7  6  5  4  3  2  1

Carol Publishing Group books are available at special discounts
for bulk purchases, for sales promotions, fund raising, or
educational purposes. Special editions can also be created to
specifications. For details contact: Special Sales Department,
Carol Publishing Group, 120 Enterprise Ave., Secaucus, NJ 07094

ISBN 0-8065-1266-0

*"...wherever you might look tonight, you might get a glimpse of me."*

("Wanted Man", Bob Dylan)

# CONTENTS

8

# Thanks & Acknowledgements

*The Telegraph*, the magazine from which the pieces in this book have been taken, wouldn't exist at all if it hadn't been for the enthusiasm of a small but happy band of friends who sat down in a pub in Manchester almost 10 years ago and decided that it would be a good idea. Thanks, then, to Graham Brandwood – who still spends too much of his spare time organising the subscriber database, Bob Carroll – who made sure we didn't go broke in the first few years, Dave Dingle – whose continued help with information is invaluable, Clinton Heylin – exhaustive archivist and abrasive commentator, John and Celia Lindley and Ian Woodward.

Neither would there be a *Telegraph* if it weren't for the subscribers, especially all those people who've spent time and money and effort in contributing articles, clippings or photographs during the last 10 years. I'm particularly grateful to all those whose work is collected in this present volume, and for their friendship and assistance through it all, Nigel Hinton, Mick Lawson, Roy Kelly, Andy O'Dwyer, Robert Schlockoff, Robert Shelton, Simon Gee, Christian Behrens, Willem Meuleman, Jeff Friedman, Bob and Susan Fino, Mitch Blank, John Hume, Michael Gray, John Hinchey, Shelly Livson, Aidan Day, Christopher Ricks, Roger Ford, Jim Dring, Barry Dickins, Albert Blenkinsop, Jill Price and all who help with distribution. For making this book possible, thanks to Simon Pettifar. For long-time friendship, thanks always to Bill Allison and Michael Krogsgaard, and for long-term sufferance, love to Penny.

I'm grateful to all those interviewed in this volume for having given up their time to talk about Bob Dylan, and acknowledgements should be made to the following people: John Pidgeon, for permission to use the text of the late Roger Scott's interview with the Traveling Wilburys; Bill Flanagan and *Musician* magazine for permission to use the Johnny Cash quotation; Allen Ginsberg for permission to edit and publish his *Renaldo & Clara* papers; Mick Kidd & Chris Garrett for permission to reprint the Biff cartoon. For photographs, thanks are due to Susan Fino, Mauro De Marco, Nancy Cleveland, Horst Mueller and Columbia Records.

Quotation has been made from the following material written and composed by Bob Dylan: Copyright by Duchess Music Corporation: Talking New York © 1962, 1965; Hard Times In New York Town © 1962, 1965; Song To Woody © 1962, 1965. Copyright by Special Rider Music, US: My Life In A Stolen Moment, In The Wind © 1973; Slow Train © 1979; Saving Grace © 1980; When The Night Comes Falling From The Sky © 1985. Used by permission. All rights reserved.

# Preface

Bob Dylan first sniffed at, then sipped from his plastic cup of whisky. As he did so he continued to squint at me through his Ray-Bans. The fact that it was almost midnight, and we were walking together down an extremely murky street, didn't seem to warrant the removal of the trademark shades. Then, with another sniff'n'swig, he paused to offer me some advice. "Make sure you tell the truth about me," he said, with surprising gravity. "A lot of people tell lies about me – make sure you tell the truth." And slowly, very deliberately – as if too much emphasis might still not be quite enough – he said it yet again, adding a final, insistent reminder, "Don't forget now – check your sources!" Then he grinned, and we walked on down the road.

Such insistence on the idea of "telling the truth" should perhaps not be surprising from one of the great creative artists of this century whose life and work have been rigorously – but more often than not pointlessly – scrutinised, and who has constantly had to suffer the slings and arrows of outrageously untruthful reporting, often idiotic criticism and constant misrepresentation, not to mention the persistent unkindness and intrusion of what he once referred to as "the dirt of gossip" and "the dust of rumour".

I'd met Bob Dylan, quite by chance, one night after a show in Hartford, Connecticut, in 1986. At that time I had been editing *The Telegraph,* a privately published magazine all about Bob Dylan, his life and his work, for more than five years. I knew he read *The Telegraph* – I'd been told that by more than one person, and anyway, although he'll tell you the opposite, Bob Dylan's always the first to know what people are writing about him – but as we sauntered down the street together, talking about a Bob Dylan show in Barcelona in 1984 that we both happened to think was wonderful, he had no way of knowing who I was. When I told him that I edited *The Telegraph*, the magazine all about him, he stopped abruptly in his tracks. Then, very slowly, he lifted up his shades and looked directly into my eyes. "Is that you?" he asked. "You do that?" "Er, yes," I replied, with curiously mixed feelings of pride and apology, wondering if I should be ready to avoid the sort of swinging punch that was later to account for Rupert Everett in *Hearts Of Fire*. "What do you think of it?" I asked, genuinely curious about what his response might be, but prepared for any eventuality. "*The Telegraph*?" he sniffed, "I seen a few issues of that. It's pretty interesting..."

That Bob Dylan should find a magazine devoted to himself "pretty interesting" is, of course, pretty funny. But Bob Dylan's a pretty funny guy, and he has some pretty funny fans, and for the best part of 10 years *The Telegraph*, which is rapidly approaching its 40th issue, has served as a kind of "clearing house" of news, opinion and information for Bob Dylan fans worldwide. It has published many articles which have assiduously – and accurately – examined crucial periods of Dylan's life and career – examined them, indeed, in far more detail than could ever be allowed in any biography, no matter how diligent the author. *The Telegraph* has also published a good deal of previously unknown information in an attempt to straighten out misconceptions and errors that might otherwise have gone unchallenged; and recent issues of the magazine have offered extensive interviews with many of Dylan's closest friends and colleagues who must have trusted *The Telegraph* not to betray their faith. All this, and the fact that, while they've never been exactly helpful, the people whose job it is to protect both Bob Dylan's privacy and his business interests have seen fit to maintain a cordial relationship with *The Telegraph* has been not only reassuring, but encouraging.

This book is the second collection of material originally published in *The Telegraph*. The first was *All Across The Telegraph*, co-edited by myself and Michael Gray and published by Sidgwick & Jackson in 1987 and Futura in 1988. Like the first collection, the present volume offers some critical assessment and occasional historical summaries, but this book has many more interviews than did the first collection, candid conversations conducted especially for *The Telegraph* and unpublished elsewhere. There's plenty to smile at along the way, lots of new perspectives on important episodes in Dylan's life, and many insights into the work, and the ways of working, of someone who, as he approaches his 50th birthday, is still writing great songs, who continues to tour with the energy and enthusiasm of a rock'n'rolling kid, and who, even after an exhilarating roller-coaster ride of a 30-year career, remains one of today's most enduring, most important, funnily idiosyncratic and constantly exciting artists.

I'm happy to be able to say that this book tells the truth about Bob Dylan.

*John Bauldie, Essex, July 1990.*

# Bobby Zimmerman in the S.A.M. Fraternity

## by John Bauldie

Bobby Zimmerman enrolled at the liberal arts college of the University Of Minnesota in September 1959. He implied, in his autobiographical poem, "My Life In A Stolen Moment"[1], that his entrance to University after what had been a rather lacklustre High School career was under somewhat dubious circumstances: "I sat in college... on a phony scholarship that I never had". "He looked awfully small-town. He dressed in an almost finicky way. He looked like Peck's Bad Boy suddenly grown five years," recalled Dr Dan Pugh, a college psychiatrist. "He acted very high-schoolish, very brash. He posed a lot, with his hand in his belt, his legs straddling the room. He wasn't big, of course, but he was heavy..."[2]

For his first few weeks in college, Bob lived, like many a clean-cut would-be scholar, in that peculiarly American student institution, a fraternity house. He moved into the predominantly Jewish Sigma Alpha Mu, 925 University Avenue Southeast, on September 29, possibly because a cousin of his, Mike Siler, a law student who was already a pledge there, had suggested to Bob's folks that "living in the fraternity would give Bob some direction." The rather seedy S.A.M. house, keen to get whatever new boarders it could, was happy to take Bob in, and Mr and Mrs Zimmerman were, one assumes, hopeful that things might work out after all, that Bobby might forget the rock'n'roll nonsense that seemed to have been preoccupying him over the last couple of years and become a lawyer like his cousin. But Bob, who'd arrived full of good intentions wearing a "typical frat uniform, narrow lapeled suit and a tie", soon found himself uncomfortable in his smart clothes and ill at ease in the company of the other "Sammies". As his father told Robert Shelton: "Bob didn't think much of the college crowd. He considered most of them phonies, just spoiled kids with whom he didn't have much in common."

Fellow Sammy Steve Bard, now a lawyer in Minneapolis, remembers Bob Zimmerman quite well:

> I remember him as being short, with a crewcut, and peach fuzz on his face. He looked like a 15-year-old high school kid who hadn't matured very much. Frankly, the impression I got of him, and which was shared by others, was that he was sorta the kinda kid you always used to pick on in high school. You know, the wimpy kid to make fun of.[3]

"He always had the same silly smile on his face that invited the others to pick on him – which they did," recalled Richard Rocklin, who had the room next to Bob's. In an unpublished piece[4], Bob writes of himself left alone in the fraternity house over Christmas, reflecting that he has little in common with his fellow boarders, who seem to think him "odd" – "I ain't even friends with any of em" – and who "chuckle" at him constantly, to his bemusement. It's remarkably confessional writing.

In another unpublished fragment, his disaffection with the fraternity house and what he considered it to represent is confirmed. He presents himself as something of a romantic figure, breaking his ties with "all things of the established order" like a young James Dean. The fraternity comes to represent or sum up "the whole established world" for Bob, and it becomes clear that he despises the fraternity, those who board there and their "jive wide smiles". "Maybe I's too sensitive..." he ponders. Bobby Zimmerman's time as a Sammy certainly wasn't a happy one.

Minnesota journalist Mark Axelrod, who conducted a survey of some of the erstwhile pledges in Minneapolis in 1979, wrote that "Few of his pledge brothers remember him being mistreated because he wasn't more active in school and in the fraternity...", but Maher Weinstein, a Minneapolis attorney, recalled that "many of the fraternity brothers were Philistines, and his interests in music and in Bohemianism seemed gauche to them." Indeed, several of the brothers were designated to "shape Zimmerman up", according to Rich Cohen, one of those chosen: "That translated into helping him make better grades, wear the right clothes and fit in." But, it seems, "though he tried to conform a little, conventionality wasn't in his blood."

It's likely that some of Bob's behaviour at this time was not just unconventional, but positively anti-social; he's remembered "pounding on the piano or beating on his guitar at odd hours of the night", and rather untunefully too, if truth be told. "If anyone tells you they saw a superstar in him then, they're full of shit," said one irritated brother. "If you would have taken a vote in the SAM house in the Spring of 1960 as to the likelihood of him succeeding in anything," said another, "you wouldn't have gotten one vote." Bob, however, "believed in himself". St Paul City Councilman Leonard Levine, another Sammy, remembers a fraternity house dance during which Bob pestered to play at the intermission. Levine, the master of ceremonies, decided to take a chance and gave the twitchy Dylan a big build-up:

> Bobby was really uptight since it was going to be his social acceptance. He sat at the piano and arranged his music, but because the lighting wasn't very good and he couldn't read his music, his performance began disastrously. I told him to forget what he wrote and play what he knew by heart, which he did, and which met with some success, but most people were not moved...

The shambolic concert didn't, one presumes, bring about the "social acceptance" that Dylan was none too actively pursuing at this time. In any case, he was already spending much more time in the local coffeehouses than he was with his fellow students...

# The Girl From The North Country

## Jaharana Romney interviewed by Markus Wittmann

*Jaharana Romney, formerly Bonnie Beecher, was – claims Robert Shelton – the "Girl From The North Country". She married Hugh Romney, aka Wavy Gravy, and currently lives in California, where she was interviewed in May, 1989.*

*Where did you meet Bob Dylan?*

I went to High School at the University of Minnesota – they had an experimental High School there called University High, and on the campus was the only beatnik cafe in the Midwest – this was in the days of the beatniks – and it was called the 10 O'Clock Scholar. I used to sneak out during my lunch hour at High School and go to the coffee house, and Dylan, who was in High School in Hibbing, used to skip school and come hitchhiking down to Minneapolis, to hang out in the one beatnik spot that we could get to. And it was in that coffeehouse that I met him.

I had an extremely esoteric record collection, quite unbelievable for an 18-year-old Minnesota girl. I had developed a taste for weird blues early in my life because of a guy in my High School class named Barry Hansen, who is now known as Dr Demento, who everybody knows! He became a music ethnocologist later in life but he was collecting records already when I was in seventh grade, so I had been turned on to blues by him when I was 11, 12, 13. Later in High School, I used to go on theatre tours to New York and I had discovered Sam Goody's record store, and I would pick out any old record that looked like it had some kind of funky singer or blues singer. There was no similar record outlet in Minnesota. There I'd buy records by Cat Iron, Rabbit Brown – I've never heard of those guys since. I had this incredible blues sophistication for an otherwise unsophisticated Minnesota girl in 1959.

Well, I went into the 10 O'Clock Scholar one day to have my bagel and apple juice, and Dylan and a guy named Harvey Abrams were sitting at the table next to me, talking about music, and I recognised some of the names. I didn't know anybody else who knew who Cat Iron was or Sleepy John Estes so I perked up my ears and turned around and I started to join the conversation. And Harvey turned to me and said to this, you know, High School senior blonde girl in a scathing kind of way, "Oh yes, I'm sure *you* know about folkies – you probably know the Kingston Trio and "The Blue And The Grey", which was the Kingston Trio's tune of the moment, and he named a bunch of the local square bands of the time, and so I was furious at this and took that opportunity to drop this list of very esoteric names of artists I was collecting, and Dylan really perked up and said, "Oh yeah? You know about *those* people? How do you know?" I said, "I've got all these records at home." The next thing I knew, Dylan and I were heading for my house. He finished up borrowing my record collection – for several years! Hahahaha!

The following year we were both freshmen at the University of Minnesota. I would go off and find a record – a collection of old blues stuff with a bunch of different artists on – bring it back to Minnesota and we would play it through and then the next time I went to New York I'd look for those names. Like, I had one album that had Bukka White on it, and Fred McDowell, and on and on, you know. I had a fantastic record collection. And Dylan would learn some of the songs he used to do before he started writing his own songs, learn them off of those old records. We played them endlessly. "Stealin'" by The Cannon City Jug Stompers was on one of them and I remember him learning that song. I remember him listening to a Rabbit Brown song, and later incorporating one of its verses into a song of his own.

The next year, my second year in college, Dylan was already in Greenwich Village, so when I went on my theatre arts tours I would duck out and go find him. I left my nice hotel and my nice High School friends, dressed myself in what I thought was appropriate to wear to go to Greenwich Village – a pair of black tights, a brown and black plaid short kilt, turtle-neck sweater – and went to join the beatnik scene with Dylan until it was time to go back to Minnesota. It was quite an adventure! Hahahaha! I got to see him at one of his first performances in Gerde's Folk City. And one of the big thrills of my life was when he took me to see Woody Guthrie.

Back in Minnesota he'd disappeared for a couple of months, he went on a trip, then he came back, talking with a real thick Oklahoma accent and wearing a cowboy hat and boots. He was into Woody Guthrie in a big big way, and I thought it was very silly because here you are, you're a Minnesota boy but you're trying to pretend to be something that you're not. But he really immersed himself in Woody Guthrie – kind of absorbed Woody. When he'd had too much to drink you'd have to call him Woody to get a response. No kidding! He was a real Woody Guthrie nut. At the time it seemed ludicrous and pretentious and foolish, but now I see it as allowing a greater Bob Dylan to come about.

When he went to New York he became one of the people who was allowed to visit Woody in hospital, but when he wrote back to Minnesota about it, no-one believed him. It was like – Hohoho! Full of crap again! Anyway, I think he took me to meet Woody Guthrie in the hospital mainly because he wanted me to go back to Minnesota and tell Harvey Abrams, Hugh Brown and Red Nelson and all the guys that he really was a friend of Woody's. Which he was! It was one of the thrills of my life.

Woody was in the insane asylum section with all these creepy people. Woody wasn't insane of course, but nobody knew who he was. I remember he wanted to play the guitar, so Dylan asked the nurse to go get his – Dylan's – guitar which had been left outside the locked gate, and the nurse who was responsible for Woody's care screamed over – it just makes my hair stand on end to think of it now – "Oh Woody! Can you play the *guitar*? Oh that's *sweet*! Here, let me look!" It was just unbelievable. The great being himself. He played "I've Been Doing Some Hard Traveling", but it was hard for him to hold the guitar because he had these spastic movements. But he struggled through it. I remember that Dylan's guitar had a sign on it that said "This machine kills fascists", which was what Woody had on his guitar. So there was Woody playing this guitar of Dylan's that had the same sign on it. And then Dylan played "Pastures Of Plenty". It was one of the greatest experiences of my life that I actually got to be in the room with Woody Guthrie, certainly one of the greatest Americans ever to have lived. And Woody loved Dylan, loved Dylan doing his songs and really appreciated that Dylan was carrying on his own kind of music in the world.

*Did you ever tape-record Bob Dylan at that time?*

Oh yes. I made several tapes of Dylan in my bedroom. People curse the recorder! It was my theatre arts teacher's little tape recorder – a reel to reel. They were stolen later and a lot of that stuff came out on the black market albums. There were 40 or 50 songs on one of the tapes. Then there was another tape made at a party, which had early versions of "Who Killed Davey Moore?" and "One Too Many Mornings". He was a little drunk. There's a very beautiful version of "Corrina Corrina" – quite inebriated and very lovely.

At that time I was living in a sorority house, until they found out that I was sleeping with a degenerate! Then they kicked me out. I didn't have the wit to deny it! Hahaha! For a while he was completely unable to support himself, and he went as far as asking to be given jobs playing just for sandwiches. I went with him to all the coffeehouses, kept trying to tell him to tell 'em, "If they'll feed you...". But no-one would let him even play for dinner. I ended up shoplifting for him, stealing food from my sorority house. This is how unfamous he was! So picture this, here's a really young guy, sitting in my bedroom in Minnesota, who no-one has ever heard of, and he sits down to make a tape, 'cos I'm sorta fond of him and fond of the music he makes and I wanna make a tape. And he says to me, "I don't want you ever to let anyone make a copy of these tapes, so that when someone from the Library Of Congress asks you for them, I want you to sell them to them for $200." What kind of a remark is *that* to make to somebody that is shoplifting food for someone who is so *incompetent* that he can't even shoplift his own food! But I promised him, and I never did let anybody make copies of those tapes. I kept that promise doggedly. And then they were stolen.

*What was his reaction when you played back the tapes after you recorded them? Did he like the way it sounded?*

The only thing I remember was that by the time I made my second or third tape he was working over "House Of The Rising Sun", and I remember him listening to it and saying, "I'm really starting to learn timing." He would sing endless long boring songs, just plod on and on with what he was trying to do regardless of the audience.

When I lived in the sorority house, we had a music room with a piano that no-one ever used. And Dylan would come and learn how to play piano there, and the harmonica. I got him his first harmonica holder at Schmidt's Music Shop – the same day I had to buy him something called Hard As Nails, a nail polish for his fingernails that made them not break. So he would come over to the sorority house and play the piano – *horribly*! And he'd play this harmonica, which he didn't know how to play! And my friends would come in and they would just go, "Uurgh! Who is this geek?" And they'd call each other up, say, "Come over here, you're not going to *believe* this!"

He was trying to learn to play two new instruments at once and he didn't care that they were making fun of him, but I was just mortified because I loved his music – I knew that he could make good music, and I remember sitting next to him saying, "Play something good! Play 'Slip Knot'! Or something that you can really do!" I wanted him to play the guitar, which he could play well and which I knew would impress them, but he just wasn't having any of it. He was saying, "Naw, I wanna get this – hwang! WHwaongg!" Hahahahaha! I was mortified, but he didn't give a shit. It's been a big lesson to me in life – just don't give a damn what people think, just go for what you are! Hahahaha! It's really the secret to life and he's one of the main people that taught it to me. Just go for it.

*When did it change around? Didn't he start to play at the 10 O'Clock Scholar?*

I was always very ambitious for him to get his act together – this was a trip I was on – so I'd say, "C'mon. Tomorrow I want you to go to four places..." And he would do that, and eventually he started playing at the Scholar. So he became known around town, and we developed a group of friends which included Koerner, Ray and Glover and Dave Morton and Dave Whitaker. He spent a lot of time at Dave Whitaker's apartment – he had this big apartment right on campus – and Whitaker was an intellectual, and we were all very impressed that he was an intellectual. Dylan credited Whitaker with teaching him the joy of reading and turning him on to books, which he had previously disdained. We were just a group of people who'd hang around and sing old gospel songs – "I'm gonna sit at the welcome table, one of these days, hallelujah" and "I thought I heard that K.C. when she moaned" – on and on, all night long. It was very nice. Glover was very James Deanish, broody and contemplative, arrogant in my opinion, but quite a musician. He was a part of the scene, but his part was that he would be aloof! He would often sit on the other side of the door, in the other room, not really joining in. But when we were singing these old gospel songs, not really blues, there would be this brilliant harmonica coming from the next room, joining in on the chorus!

Dylan's early voice...do you know his voice on *Nashville Skyline*? It's sort of different from the rest of his...well, Dylan's early voice sounded like that. I was startled when I heard him again on *Nashville Skyline*. He got this bronchial cough that lasted almost a year, and it was very very bad. I kept trying to drag him down to the health service but he wouldn't do it. It was still his "I wanna be Woody Guthrie" stage and he wouldn't take care of it because he thought the rougher his voice sounded, the more he was gonna sound like Woody Guthrie. I thought that as a result of the year of the bronchial cough he had lost his ability to have that sweet voice altogether, until I heard it again on *Nashville Skyline*.

*Was he doing any studying at all at the time?*

Yeah, we did some studying. We were in the astronomy class together and we once stayed up and studied almost all night because we both had an astronomy final, and I had a theatre arts final. He also had this music theory final and he got himself pretty drunk the night before and I was getting worried about his ability to go and take it. I was yapping at him, "Music is your life! You need to study! Yap yap yap!" We stayed up together until five o'clock in the morning and then I slipped out back to my sorority – I'd stuck a playing card in the back door so I could get back in – and two hours later I was back out, on my way to take my final exam. But I was thinking about how I'd left him and I was worried that he wouldn't be able to make it to his music exam because he had got himself so drunk.

Anyway, I was walking to the building where I had my final and I noticed a crowd standing around. Sure enough, Dylan was lying in the middle of the street and – just a *mess*, you know? He had thrown up and he was passed out on the street and his clothes were all... And I remember thinking, "I could just keep walking. Hahahaha! I don't *have* to go in there and say I know this person. Hahahaha!" But I took a big sigh, knew I was going to be late for my test, and dammit I went in and picked him up, he was barely conscious, walked him into the Theatre Arts building where all my friends were, and I had this ludicrous drunk hanging on me,

23

covered in vomit! I walked him into the ladies' room, cleaned him up, and I wanted to take him home, but he said, "Naw! I have to be at the Music building!" So I said, "Well, OK." So I walked him to the Music building, we went downstairs – he could hardly make the stairs – and I sat him down at one of those seats that had a place in front of it and left him there. I went off to take my test.

He got a C at that final! I couldn't believe it! I can't believe it to this day! He couldn't hold a pencil! He couldn't even see hardly. Maybe music was so much a part of him that he didn't need to be able to read to pass that final exam – it's just one of the big miracles!

*I wanted to ask you about Dylan and his fraternity house.*

Well, he didn't live there long. I have a vague memory of being told by Dylan that his father didn't want to pay for the fraternity any more, because there was some conflict about his father wanting him to use the name Zimmerman and Dylan refusing to use the name Zimmerman, but I could be wrong about that. Eventually he was ousted from the fraternity under some circumstances that made him uncomfortable to talk about it and I don't think I ever got the straight story. He told me both that his father wouldn't pay and that they threw him out. I don't know which one is true.

I remember some time later, I had been thrown out of my sorority and he came back after his first year in New York and did a concert at the students' union at the University of Minnesota and there was a real good review of it, and he had his record out and so on. I remember him saying that he had gone to his old fraternity house, Sigma Alpha Mu, and a big sign was hanging up on the board saying, "Bob Dylan – Our Alumni Makes Good!" And he was really furious because they had kicked him out and now he was becoming famous they wanted to claim him, take credit for him. It was the height of hypocrisy.

*Did he write any original songs back in Minnesota?*

Well, it's hard to say. He was doing some writing. There was a song called, "I Was Young When I Left Home" – he said he wrote that. I think he wrote it. He wrote "Song To Woody" quite early – he may still have been in Minnesota when he wrote that. He wrote a couple of fooling around songs – he wrote one when I cut his hair, which made me so angry!

He came to my apartment and said, "It's an emergency! I need your help! I gotta go home an' see my mother!" He was talking in the strangest Woody Guthrie-Oklahoma accent. I don't know if she was sick, but it was an unexpected trip he had to make up to Hibbing and he wanted me to cut his hair "real short, real short so that she won't know that I wear long hair." He kept saying, "Shorter! Shorter! Get rid of the sideburns!" So I did my very best to do what he wanted and then in the door come Dave Morton, Johnny Koerner and Harvey Abrams. They looked at him and said, "Oh my God, you look terrible! What did you do?" And Dylan immediately said, "She did it! I told her just to trim it up a little bit but she cut it all off. I wasn't looking in a mirror!" And then he went and wrote that song, "Bonnie, why'd you cut my hair? Now I can't go nowhere!" He played it that night in a coffeehouse and somebody told me recently that they had been to Minnesota and somebody was still playing that song, "Bonnie, Why'd You Cut My Hair?"[5] It's like a Minnesota classic! And so I've gone down in history!

# Bob Dylan in New York – January to April 1961

## by John Bauldie

A four-door Pontiac is just leaving the Hudson tunnel. It has carried five people from Madison, Wisconsin to New York City. It's late afternoon on Tuesday, January 24, 1961 and the snow is driving across the highway. The windscreen wipers are flipping and flapping too slowly to properly clear the snowflakes. In the back seat are two new friends. The car is warm and New York is cold. There are snowdrifts piled along the avenues, cars ploughed in, and everything is frozen. The wipers continue their too slow flip-flap as the car moves through upper Manhattan. One of the back seat passengers is dozing, another, wide-eyed and wide awake, eager and excited, is looking at the buildings and the cars, the signs on the street corners, the subways, the restaurants, the trashcans, and everywhere the snow. So much snow – the worst snow since 1933. This wide-eyed boy is 19 years old but looks a couple of years younger. He is both curious and a curiosity in his pea jacket, work shirt and old and baggy trousers that have been turned up and turned down again. He wears once-suede boots that must have seen a thousand miles of walking. His jacket collar is turned up. He has a funny black cord cap that perches on his curly hair. He has the face of an angel.

It's late afternoon in the autumn of 1985. Two men are talking. One draws on a cigarette, blows the smoke out to the left, pinches the end of the filter-tip and looks beyond the other towards the past: "I knew I had to get to New York ... I'd been dreaming about that for a long time."

The listener duly notes these words. He has recorded them on a cassette tape. Sometime later they will be underlined and typed. They will be read and re-read and then typed again. A screen will display the words in a lurid green light. The speaker takes another draw on the cigarette and looks at his hands. He is 44 years old. The listener looks at his face. It communicates experience rather than age. It is a face worn by thought, a singular face.

A woman called Jennifer Warren, speaking in 1970, recalls a conversation she had 10 years earlier in Madison, Wisconsin: "He told us he was going to hit the Village ... he was going to New York so he could sit by Woody's bedside because Woody was dying. He said he was planning to see him in the hospital in New Jersey."[6]

Bob Dylan had stopped off in Madison on his way back to Minnesota from Chicago. There he met the kids who were moving East: "They needed two people to help drive to New York and that's how I felt. Me and a guy named Fred Underhill went with them. Fred was from Williamstown or somewhere and he knew New York."[7]

> *I had my guitar an' harmonica to play*
> *An' he had his brother's clothes to pawn*
> *In a week, he went back to Madison while I*
> *stayed behind an'*
> *Walked a winter's line from the Lower East Side*
> *to Gerde's Folk City*
> ("My Life In A Stolen Moment")

The car must have dropped Dylan and Fred Underhill uptown – "up around Sixty-second Street" according to "Talkin' Folklore Center", an unrecorded early song.

A week before Dylan's arrival in New York the snow had started to fall:

> *Snow was piled up the stairs*
> *an onto the street that first*
> *winter when i laid around New York City*
> ("In The Wind")

"Slush in my boots all winter long wandering around the Village. Cold winter – snow that high," he gestured, arms describing the biggest snowbank since the blizzard of '33.[8]

> *Wintertime in New York town*
> *The wind blowin snow around*
> *Walk around with nowhere to go*
> *Somebody could freeze right to the bone*
> *I froze right to the bone*
> ("Talkin' New York")

Where I came from there was always plenty of snow so I was used to that, but going to New York was like going to the moon. You just didn't get on a plane and go there, you know. New York! Ed Sullivan, the New York Yankees, Broadway, Harlem... you might as well have been talking about China... It was some place which not too many people had ever gone, and anybody who did go never came back...[9]

## TUESDAY, JANUARY 24, 1961

*I came down to New York town*
*Got out and started walking around*
*I's up around sixty-second street*
*All of a sudden comes a cop on his beat*
*Said my hair was too long, said my boots were too dirty,*
*Said my hat was un-American, said he'd throw me in jail.*
*So I got on a subway...*
("Talkin' Folklore Centre")

*I swung on to my old guitar*
*Grabbed hold of a subway car*
*After a rocking, reeling, rolling ride,*
*I landed up on the downtown side*
*Greenwich Village.*
("Talkin' New York")

Bobby Dylan stumbled into the Cafe Wha?

It was a grubby, awful scene there. It was a basket house. We were all treated like shit. The customers were tourists. I slept on floors a lot. It was a desperate struggle there. I guess like a lot of others I was enthralled by the idea of living the Kerouac life – just me and my guitar. I liked playing blues guitar more than anything else in the world, but there was just no money in it there ...[10]

Not Bob Dylan but David Barry. This is Bob Dylan:

I used to play in a place called Cafe Wha? and it always used to open at noon. It opened at noon and it closed at six in the morning and it was just a non-stop flow of people. Usually they were tourists who were looking for Beatniks in the Village. There used to be maybe five groups that played there. I used to play with a guy called Fred Neil... I would just play harmonica with him. And once in a while I would get to sing a song, y'know, when he was taking a break or something. And so I'd get to sing a song once, and play harmonica the rest of the time. That was his show. He'd be on maybe a half-hour, and then a conga drum group called Los Congeros with 20 conga drum players and bongos, and they would play for maybe half an hour. And then this girl – I think her name was Judy Rainey – she used to play sweet southern mountain Appalachian ballads with an electric guitar and a small amplifier. And then another guy used to sing on there named Hal Lauders. He used to be a crooner, used to sound like Leon Bibb – remember him? – and then there'd be a comedian! And he'd go up for maybe 15 or 20 minutes. And then an impersonater. And that'd be the whole show. This unit would be... would just go around, non-stop, so you'd know where you went on, after whoever it was. And then you could eat there then, which was actually the best thing about the place. Then go back on. The comedian would be on until he was hooted off the stage. If they didn't like you back then, you couldn't play! If they liked you, you played more. And if they didn't like you, you didn't play at all. You played one or two songs and people would just boo or hiss or something.[11]

When Dylan first blew through the door in a flurry of snowflakes, he found the place half-empty. It was the regular Tuesday hootenanny, and the owner, Manny Roth, may have been trying to outstare a half-empty register when a half-real angel-demon appeared unto him. With a headful of Guthrie ideas, Bob Dylan took the stage in New York City for the very first time, playing a short set of Woody Guthrie songs, offering tales of his own wanderings along Woody Guthrie's roads. There was an appreciative response to Dylan's charismatic, pie-eyed appeal. It must have sounded like heroic acclaim to the excited kid: "They flipped... I played there and they flipped. They really did."[12]

When he heard that this chubby faced kid had nowhere to sleep, the club owner helped – or tried to – by asking from the stage if anyone could give him a bed for the night. In the Billy James interview, Dylan, recalling a self-confident bravado that he may not actually have shown, says he made the request himself, figuring that the response to his performance had been so enthusiastic that super-hospitality was guaranteed; it would be a privilege for whoever offered:

I figured if they liked me so much that maybe someone would have a place to stay the night. So I asked from the stage, and about four hands went up... My buddy and I, we sort of went and checked 'em out, picked out this fellow who was with a girl. Then my buddy says to me, 'He don't look so hot, and I don't think ... he don't look so hot. He looks pretty gay.' And I said 'He looks OK' – and anyway, he was with a girl. And so we went up with him. And the girl got off at 34th Street, and we got off at 42nd Street! Well, we went in a bar before we went to find this place to stay, and we met his friend 'Dora'. 'Dora' was his friend who stayed with him. And both of us looked, and ran out of the bar really – ran out like anything![13]

Where Bob Dylan and Fred Underhill ended up that first night, no-one seems to remember. Dylan's first official CBS biography says he slept in subways for his first few nights in New York. If he ever did (his mother told Toby Thompson that "Bob had connections in New York") the cold night of January 24, 1961 is as likely a date as any for Bob Dylan to have found himself subterraneanly homesick.

WEDNESDAY, JANUARY 25, 1961

As Dylan's primary purpose in getting to New York was to visit Woody Guthrie, it's highly likely that he took off for New Jersey the day after his arrival. In his book *Woody Guthrie – A Life*, Joe Klein tells of Dylan phoning the hospital several times and being told that Mr Guthrie couldn't come to the telephone. The hospital did confirm, however, that Woody was always pleased to see visitors.

Woody had been in bad physical shape for some time. The hereditary Huntington's Chorea – a disease which had claimed his mother – had been diagnosed in Woody in September 1952, and the deterioration in him over the following years makes for painful reading. At the end of May 1956, Woody had been arrested for vagrancy but, clearly a sick man, he had been taken to Greystone Park, a massive State institution as bleak as its name, in Morris Plains, New Jersey. He would remain there for the next five years: "He called it 'Gravestone' and panicked when be learned that he was stuck there. Because his admission hadn't exactly been voluntary, he couldn't check himself out..."[14] Not just that, but nobody seemed to care for him any more, as one of his letters attests:

> Six biggy loney somey hard months here since I seed any or alla you o god please justa donty ya ever let me suffer this lonesome without you way this long no more... and I do really die from my loneysomeness here when you guys in my gang there just never do ever writey me no letters here nor drop over ta see me... So how now would you feel if you are me if you was me 6 months in here and notta dam dam dam vizitor off no dam kind...

Friends did begin to come to see Woody, who was slowly but surely dying. By the end of 1960:

His physical condition had deteriorated markedly ... the little twitches and shakes had become gross, unpredictable lurches of his arms and legs and torso. Despite heavy medication, he was in constant motion. The worst of it seemed to be his right arm, which would fly up and strike his forehead with such force that sometimes, when they hadn't clipped his nails at the hospital, he'd gash himself with his thumb and blood would pour down his face ...He was still able to walk but he looked like he was walking across a trampoline. His speech was a slurred, guttural rumble and difficult to understand if you weren't used to it. He never spoke much, in any case, and occasionally seemed to slip into a sort of trance, and no-one could reach him. Usually though his mind was very clear...[15]

This, then, was the Woody Guthrie who would receive 19-year-old Bob Dylan on this cold January afternoon.

In the fall of 1960, looking for a focus for his music and for his identity, Dylan had been introduced to Woody's music and to his book, *Bound For Glory*, in Minneapolis, by David Whitaker. In the Westwood One radio interview, Dylan recalled that time:

I heard Woody Guthrie and then it all came together for me ... His songs really impressed me because they were original. They had the mark of originality on them, the lyrics did. I just learned all those songs. I heard them and I learned them all off the records. I learned all the songs of Woody Guthrie that I could find. Anybody that had a Woody Guthrie record or that knew a Woody Guthrie song – and in St Paul at the time where I was, there were some people around who not only had his records but knew his songs. So I just learned 'em all ...[16]

Within weeks, Dylan had soaked up as much as he could of Guthrie's songs. In December, Whitaker mentioned that he'd read in *Sing Out!* about Woody being in hospital in New Jersey, and Dylan immediately upped and left:

I was pretty fanatical about what I wanted to do, so after learning about 200 of Woody's songs, I went to see him and I waited for the right moment to visit him in a hospital in Morristown, New Jersey. I took a bus from New York, sat with him and sang his songs.[17]

The visit was clearly hugely exciting. Dylan sent a postcard off to the Whitakers:

The card carried the classic photo of Woody in a workshirt, holding his guitar in front of him. Dylan's enthusiasm leaps off the card: "I know Woody. I know Woody... I know him and met him and saw him and sang to him. I know Woody – Goddamn." He signed it "Dylan".[18]

## THURSDAY, JANUARY 26, 1961

It seems likely that while he had been with Woody Guthrie, Dylan had learned that every Sunday Guthrie was taken to the home of Bob and Sidsel Gleason in New Jersey, on North Arlington Avenue, East Orange. The day after visiting Guthrie, Dylan went out to East Orange to meet the Gleasons, and to fix an invitation for himself for the weekend:

He said little except that he loved Woody and wanted to spend time with him. He looked like an archangel almost, like a choirboy, with that little round face and the beautiful eyes. His hair in those days was long and curly and he wore that dark Eton cap. He had a pair of boots that was two sizes too big; everything that child had was either too small or too big. He bought a jacket for instance that didn't fit him at all. I think he paid 75 cents for it in one of those Village thrift shops.[19]

The Sunday visit having been fixed, Dylan sent off the postcard to the Whitakers, telling them that he would soon be sitting around with Woody, Jack Elliott, Cisco Houston and Will Geer. Now he had another visit to make.

## FRIDAY, JANUARY 27, 1961

After East Orange, next stop Queens, and the Guthries' house in Howard Beach. Bob Dylan probably went there on the Friday of his first week in New York:

It's not clear why he did so, probably just anxious to learn as much as he could about Woody and his family. He rang the bell and a teenage girl opened the door.
"I came to look for Woody," he told her
"He's in the hospital."
"You his daughter?" he asked
"No, I'm the babysitter," she replied.
"Hey, can I come in and say hello to the kids?"[20]

The babysitter insisted on phoning Marjorie Guthrie, who was at her dancing school. Mrs Guthrie told her not to let him in, the "awful strange looking kid" described to her over the phone, but 13-year-old Arlo had already intervened:

> The babysitter wanted to send him away but I let him in. I liked him because he was wearing boots and looked interesting. We talked for a few minutes and he showed me how to play a few tunes on the harmonica. He showed me how to play it in the other key than it is.[21]

When Marjorie Guthrie got home from work she found a houseful of bubbling children:

> The children told me about the fabulous, wonderful visit they had had with this odd-looking boy. I could tell from the children's response to him that he was probably a warm, kindly and talented kid.[22]

## SATURDAY, JANUARY 28, 1961

> *On MacDougal Street I saw a cubby hole*
> *I went in to get out of the cold*
> *Found out after I entered*
> *The place was called the Folklore Center*
> *Owned by Izzy Young....*
> ("Talkin' Folklore Center")

The central day-to-day meeting place for almost everyone connected with the emergent folk-scene in the Village was the Folklore Center, at 110 MacDougal between Bleeker and West 3rd Street:

> It wasn't a very big place – a couple of narrow rooms strung together. The records and books were out front. There were instruments on the walls, and there were a lot of people generally milling around...[23]

Founded in March 1957 by Izzy Young (a larger than life figure, described by Eric Von Schmidt in his book *Baby Let Me Follow You Down* as "loud, energetic, disorganised, petty, big-hearted, and totally dedicated to serving the cause of folk-music and folk-singers"), the Folklore Center was a positive treasure-house for the folk crowd, packed with all kinds of instruments, folk records, songbooks, magazines, picks and strings; it was a meeting place and a booking agency, a place to make connections – one wall of the 10-feet-wide room being a community bulletin board for announcements – and a place to learn. Jim Rooney recalls his first visit to the Folklore Center, and his first meeting with Izzy Young:

> Izzy was on the phone. The word 'schmuck' came up frequently. His hair was all over the place. His nose was very big. His shirt was rumpled and coming out his pants. He had big glasses on. His accent was a caricature of every New York Jew I'd ever dreamed of. I was just sort of browsing around and I immediately picked up on a Bill Clifton songbook which had about 300 country and bluegrass songs in it. No-one but Izzy would have had that in the North at that time.

Izzy Young asked Rooney if he knew Dylan:

> We went into the back room and there was Dylan sitting at a cluttered desk, banging away on a typewriter. Izzy told him who we were and where we were from. He immediately handed me a bunch of sheets with songs on them. I mean a bunch. He was writing like a man possessed. His feet were bouncing up and down up and down as he talked. He was on fire.[24]

What seems to have been Dylan's first visit to the Folklore Center was recalled by Jack R. Goddard in the *Village Voice:*

> Picking up an autoharp, he began mumbling a song about some bloke named Captain Gray. People looked on in amusement as he began hopping around a bit. He was funny to watch, and anybody with half an ear could tell he had a unique style. But few could have guessed on that wintry morning that a real *enfant terrible* had arrived on the folk music scene, or that within a single year he would emerge as one of the most gifted and unusual entertainers in the whole country.

SUNDAY, JANUARY 29, 1961

Sometime in 1959, Bob Gleason, a New Jersey electrician, and his wife Sidsel, heard a radio programme about Woody Guthrie. They were both long-time Guthrie fans, and when they heard that Woody was at the nearby Greystone Park Hospital they visited him. After several such visits, they started bringing him to their home at weekends – and word quickly spread through the New York folk community that Woody was receiving visitors on Sundays in East Orange – an easy bus ride from the city. Proceedings would start about noon; Marjorie and the kids would be there, Pete Seeger as often as not, Alan Lomax, and a handful of the younger folkie enthusiasts including John Cohen and Peter La Farge. Bob Dylan went out there on Sunday, January 29. Cisco Houston and Jack Elliott may well have been there too. Joe Klein, in his biography of Woody Guthrie, writes of Rambling Jack spending a whole afternoon "hiding his face under a pushed-down cowboy hat and crying as he played all of Woody's old favourites..."

Another person present on that same afternoon was Camilla Dams Horne. She recalls Dylan spending most of the day sitting on the floor beside the couch on which Woody was sprawled out:

> That first time, Bob didn't say a word for a long while. He was just sitting there most of the time, very quietly. I remember he kept that cap on. And finally he did sing something, and it was impressive...it was probably one of Woody's. And I do remember that night Woody saying, 'He's a talented boy. Gonna go far.'[25]

Dylan was soon to move in with the Gleasons, and he shared further Sunday afternoons with Woody Guthrie. In *Woody Guthrie – A Life*, Joe Klein remarks:

> A real rapport seemed to develop between Woody and Dylan, with Woody often asking the Gleasons if 'the boy' was going to be there on Sunday. 'That boy's got a voice,' he told them, 'maybe he won't make it with his writing, but he can sing it...'

FEBRUARY, 1961

> *Well, it's up in the mornin' tryin' to find a job of work*
> *Stand in one place till your feet begin to hurt...*
> *...it's hard times in the city,*
> *Livin' down in New York Town.*
> ("Hard Times In New York Town")

New York was a dream... It was a dream of the cosmopolitan riches of the mind. It was a great place for me to learn and to meet others who were on similar journeys.[26]

When Dylan... arrived in New York... he banged smack dab and kerplunk into a vast myriad of pyrotechnics and pressures, and for a boy who was from some real corkscrew town way out in the western forests or something, the new scene must have been difficult to digest so rapidly. And now Dylan... had some fast moves to make; and if there was one thing that Dylan could do, it was change. He assessed the new scene, very quickly and accurately, and moved with speed to conquer what he had fallen on... He talked about running away from his home in Duluth and he walked down the streets in suede and dungarees, curled against snow and cold... Still, I paid attention to him because he generated some mystical powers; one somehow recognised that within this frail young man there burned some kind of raw dynamic inspiration.[27]

Dylan played at a coffeehouse called The Commons during the first week of February. Peter Stampfel was to see him playing the same club sometime later:

I assumed he was a punk motorcycle type because he wore this punk motorcycle type hat... but he didn't look like a motorcycle punk when he moved with that guitar... talk about having your mind blown – that same incredible rush as when I heard Little Richard for the first time, in 1956. He started his set with a fiddly banjo-type tune called "Sally Ann", which just about took the top of my head off. He was doing all traditional songs, but it was his approach! His singing style and phrasing were stone rhythm and blues – he fitted the two styles together perfectly, clear as a bell, and I realised for the first time that my two true loves, traditional music and rock music, were in fact one. They were one! People who heard him back then often go on about how bad he used to sound; he sounded great then; it just took them a long time to learn how to listen.[28]

Dylan sent the Whitakers a further postcard, telling them he had been playing at The Commons: "People clap for me," he reported, encouraged. He also told them that he saw Woody four times a week, and that "Woody likes me – he tells me to sing for him – he's the greatest holiest godliest one in the world."

On an afternoon in early February 1961, Woody's friends gathered to play some music for him at One Sheridan Square, the Greenwich Village nightclub that formerly had been Cafe Society. Lee Hays remembered Cisco Houston walking in, riddled with cancer, and seeing Woody there, shaking so badly that he barely could hold on to his seat:

Cisco went over to him and kissed Woody on the forehead, and Woody, who was always such a macho sort and never much for physical contact, seemed to lift his head up in order to be kissed. It was a stunning moment.[29]

Bob Dylan is almost certain to have been there. On the Westwood One radio interview Dylan recalled Cisco Houston:

One of the biggest thrills I had actually when I reached New York – whenever it was – I got to play with Cisco Houston. I did get to play with him at a party or something. He was an amazing looking guy. I mean he looked like Clark Gable. He was a movie star... one of the great unsung heroes of all time, one of the great American figures; and you ask people, and no-one knows anything about him.

Cisco Houston died some 10 weeks later, on April 29, 1961.

SUNDAY, FEBRUARY 12, 1961

Dylan was round at the Gleasons' again in company with Woody and the regular crowd. Also there were Barbara Shutner and her husband:

> My husband Logan English and I met Bob Dylan at Bob and Sid Gleason's house... One night we were all sitting around and Woody said something like, 'Play something' to this kid sitting on the couch. The kid was Bob Dylan, and he sang and it was just beautiful. So Logan said, 'I'm working at Gerde's. I'm the MC. We'll get you to play there.' So that Monday night, Bob came in and did his first set.

It's quite likely, then, that Dylan played at the Hootenanny at Gerde's Folk City for the first time on Monday, February 13, 1961:

> In came this funny-looking kid one night, dressed as if he had just spent a year riding freight trains, and playing songs in a style that you could tap your feet to. Dylan's early style was a combination of blues, rock and country which caught on the very minute that he stepped on the stage at Gerde's.

It's interesting, isn't it, that Dylan's tongue-in-cheek account of his rejection by the club owner in "Talkin' New York" has its source in truth. Dylan just didn't sound anything like a Greenwich Village folk-singer. When he tries to sound like a folk-singer – as on "Young But Growing" for example – he sounds slightly ridiculous; but when he sounds like a hillbilly, with his Hank Williams moans, Woody Guthrie licks, Jimmie Rodgers whoops and Little Richard cries, he makes all the regular folk-singers sound ridiculous. There never had been anyone like him. Among those impressed by Dylan-at-first-sight was Tom Paxton:

> It was a Hootenanny at Gerde's. Van Ronk and I were sitting together and this kid got up and sang and we both thought that he was just marvellous – no limit to his potential.[30]

Another spectator in Gerde's was Nat Hentoff:

My wife and I used to live around the corner from Gerde's Folk City and we were very much interested by the whole folk-song scene at the time. We used to start dropping into Gerde's on Monday nights when they had the so-called Hootenannies, where people would try out their stuff. And there's this scrawny kid whose voice at first I couldn't stand. It had nothing to do with any of the criteria of sounds that I was used to. I don't mean the fact that it wasn't 'attractive'. I just didn't think it was at all musical. But there was something about him, a kind of insistent presence...[31]

If it wasn't Dylan's music which had the magnetism then, it was something about him which engaged an audience. It must have been quite an experience to see this incarnation of Bob Dylan. Joan Baez:

It was in Gerde's Folk City and he was singing his "Song To Woody". And he knocked me out completely. As I remember him, it seems he was about five feet tall: he seemed tiny, just tiny, with that goofy little hat on... and he was just astounding. I was knocked out, totally absorbed by his style, and his eyes and the whole mystical whatever it was, and I just thought about him for days. I was amazed, and I was happy. He really made me happy that there was somebody with that kind of talent. I'm really hooked on geniuses and any time it happens along I really get excited.[32]

*Time* magazine was there too:

There he stands, and who can believe him? Black corduroy cap, green corduroy shirt, blue corduroy pants. Hard lick guitar, whooping harmonica, skinny little voice. Beardless chin, shaggy sideburns, porcelain pussy cat eyes... he looks 14, and his accent belongs to a jive Nebraskan, or maybe a Brooklyn hillbilly.[33]

Robert Shelton:

He was so astonishing looking, so Chaplinesque and cherubic, sitting on a stool playing the guitar and the harmonica and playing with the audience, making all kinds of wry faces, wearing this Huck Finn cap, that I laughed out loud with pleasure. I called over Pat Clancy and he looked at the cherub and broke into a broad smile and said, 'Well, what have we here?'[34]

Robert Shelton was to see a great deal of Bob Dylan in the coming months:

We used to knock around listening to music together, and that period was interesting because Dylan was listening to every bit of music he could hear. He walked around with his ears hanging out, eager to follow whatever was going on in folk music. He'd come over to my house and play piano and listen to records.[35]

The Ribakoves:

There were parties that ran all night long in someone's East Village loft or basement pad. There were new faces appearing in the folk music world and the price of a cup of coffee or a welcome at the Folklore Center would give even the brokest a chance to see and hear and discuss the new talent. It was a generous world, more apt to praise – and to help – a green kid than to jeer. It was an active world... a good world for a young 'hard-to-get-along-with' genius to grow in, to experiment, and expand...[36]

Arthur Kretchmer, a young magazine editor, remembers meeting Dylan at a party:

There was this crazy restless little kid sitting on the floor and coming on very strong about how he was going to play Holden Caulfield in a movie of *Catcher In The Rye*, and I thought, 'This kid is really terrible'. But the people whose party it was said, 'Don't let him put you off. He comes on a little strong, but he's very sensitive, writes poetry, goes to visit Woody Guthrie in the hospital.' And I figured right, another one![37]

But of course he wasn't just another one. In Scaduto's *Bob Dylan,* Mikki Isaacson recalls a similar party, but a very different Dylan. He had been brought to her small apartment by Johnny Herald of The Greenbriar Boys:

Bobby sat on the floor that first time, very shabby-looking... He was slouching, looking so uncomfortable and ill-at-ease, I kind of felt he didn't want anybody to know he was there. He didn't say a word. He didn't have a thing to say. One of the boys, maybe Herald or maybe Van Ronk, said to me, 'You really ought to hear this kid sing', and I thought, 'Boy he's probably a mess.' They tried to persuade him to sing, worked on him. I felt he was insecure, so I said, 'I'd really like to hear you,' and he came out of his shell. He moved toward the group, sat on the edge of one of the chairs, and began to play. He didn't even have his own guitar with him: he borrowed someone else's. And he sang a song about somebody's death, and I wept. I was just undone by it. He sang it almost as if he was singing for himself, not for the rest of us. And all of these people there, all these professionals, they made it clear they thought Bobby was something special, that he really had it. He knocked everyone out.[38]

Gil Turner, in *The Folk Rock Story*, speaks of Dylan at this time:

> His flair for the comic gesture and the spontaneous quip, the ability to relate his thoughts on practically any subject from hitchhiking to the phoniness of Tin Pan Alley, and make it entertaining, make Bob's stage personality. It is not a contrived, play-acted personality. One gets the impression that his talk and storytelling on stage are things that just come into his head that he thought you might be interested in.[39]

Here's another recollection:

> On one occasion, while on stage, he looked at himself in the mirror which stood behind the bar at Gerde's. He combed his hair and declared sarcastically how handsome he was, and then, as if all this didn't happen, went right on with one of his songs. He had this rare ability of laughing at himself and at the same time putting across serious material.[40]

Robert Shelton was to make exactly the same oberservations in his article, *The Charisma Kid:*

> He was only 19 then, looking, with his thin pale face, as if parts of a choirboy and parts of a beatnik had gone astray in one of the tunnels from Jersey and been hastily reassembled before the Manhattan exit... In the village clubs, Dylan touched his audience occasionally with his bluesy songs and his emerging poetic statements, but mostly he made them laugh. He had a curious set of Charlie Chaplin tramp mannerisms that were irresistible. His shamble would send him way past the target of the microphone, and there was a lot of stage business with his hat, his hair, his harmonica.[41]

Surprising as it may seem now, the Charlie Chaplin comparison is to recur whenever those early club appearances are remembered, and Dylan himself confirmed Chaplin's influence on him in the Billy James interview:

> My biggest idol on stage I think, even off stage, running all through my head all the time was Charlie Chaplin, and... er... this takes a while to explain but I mean... he's one of *the* men.[42]

40

*I'm out here a thousand miles from my home*
*Walkin' a road other men have gone down*
*I'm seein' your world of people and things*
*Your paupers and peasants and princes and kings.*
*Hey, hey, Woody Guthrie, I wrote you a song..."*
("Song To Woody")

In the Westwood One radio interview, Dylan said:

I was playing Woody Guthrie's stuff when I came to New York.
That's all I was playing – Woody Guthrie songs... and then one day I
just wrote a song. The first song I ever wrote that I performed in
public was the song I wrote to Woody Guthrie.

Scaduto comments:

The Gleasons have a sheet of yellow ruled legal paper, and on it, in
Dylan's tight but somewhat sloppy handwriting, is 'A Song To
Woody'. At the bottom of this copy he wrote: 'Written by Bob Dylan
in Mills' Bar on Bleeker Street in New York City on the 14th day of
February, for Woody Guthrie.'

Dylan explained the song's composition in a paragraph which
accompanied its first publication in *Sing Out!* magazine, under the
title "Letter To Woody":

It was written in the 1960th winter...in New York City in the drug
store on 8th Street. It was on one of them freezing days that I came
back from Sid and Bob Gleason's in East Orange, New Jersey...
Woody was there that day and it was a February Sunday night... and
I just thought about Woody; I wondered about him, thought harder
and wondered harder... I wrote this song in five minutes... it's all I
got to say... If you know anything at all about Woody then you'll
know what I'm tryin to say...if you don't know anything about
Woody, then find out.

"Song To Woody" was the first song that Dylan had written that
he regularly performed in the clubs. In the next few months he
would begin to write profusely. As he commented in the *Spin*
interview of December 1985:

I began writing because I was singing. I think that's an important
thing. I started writing because things were changing all the time
and a certain song needed to be written. I started writing them
because I wanted to sing them. Anyway, one thing led to another

and I just kept on writing my own songs, but I stumbled into it really. It was nothing I had prepared myself for, but I did sing a lot of songs before I wrote any of my own. I think that's important too.

## MONDAY, APRIL 3, 1961

Dylan had been living with whoever would take him in – at times with Dave Van Ronk, occasionally with Rambling Jack Elliott, a week here, a week there, a crash pad at 629 East 5th Street with an anonymous folkie girl who played a lyre, then with Avril, a dancer and an actress who had seen him at Folk City and fallen for him. He was with Avril on East 4th Street for the last few weeks of his first time in New York. He continued to play gigs, but Gerde's was the most important. Dylan showed up for hoots regularly and soon had a following there. Mike Porco could see that the audience liked him even though he was still a little puzzled by their enthusiasm. Still, at the prompting of Robert Shelton and a couple called Mel and Lillian Bailey, Mike Porco decided that Dylan was worth a paying gig – two weeks' residency supporting John Lee Hooker: "He was so excited he was jumping up and down. His first real job, and working with John Lee Hooker who was liked by everybody."[43]

But Dylan needed a union card if he was to be a professional performer. The fee was $46, and Dylan was flat broke. Porco suggested that he take the money out of the wage for the two weeks' work – Dylan was to be paid $100 – and on Monday, April 3, Porco took Dylan down to the union office:

> The man gave Bob the contract and asked him to fill it out, and when he filled in the age as 19 the union secretary said, 'I can't OK this because you're under 21. Come in tomorrow with your father.' Bob says, 'I got no father.' The union man says, 'Come in with your mother,' and Bob says, 'I got no mother either.' Bob was sitting in the centre between us and the union man leans back behind him and forms the words in his mouth, asking me, 'Is he a bastard?' and I said, 'I don't know.' Then he suggested I sign it as a guardian, and I did. Bob got his union book.[44]

The union book cost him half of his wages.

## TUESDAY, APRIL 11, 1961

Dylan looked a little strange when he took the stage at Gerde's Folk City for his major professional debut. He'd had a haircut, and he was wearing odd clothes – a pair of old slacks, borrowed, and – proudly – one of Woody Guthrie's jackets, given to him by Sid

Gleason. Woody couldn't be there, but Dylan sang "Song To Woody", and carried himself with an authority that belied his years. He was 19 years old, and he was "something special, possibly a genius".[45] He had been in New York for 76 days.

# BOB DYLAN

### Exclusively on Columbia Records

"In his first album, accompanying himself on guitar and taking an occasional whooping break on the harmonica, Dylan plunges into Negro blues, plaintive mountain songs, updated Scottish tunes and sardonic folklike pieces of his own composition. He adapts his sound and phrasing to the varying needs of the material, but throughout he is unabashedly himself. Among his other accomplishments, Dylan is expert in the 'talking blues' popularized by Woody Guthrie, a friend and major influence."

**Nat Hentoff, The Reporter, May 24, 1962**

"Resembling a cross between a choir boy and a beatnik, Mr. Dylan has a cherubic look and a mop of tousled hair he partly covers with a Huck Finn black corduroy cap. His clothes may need a bit of tailoring, but when he works his guitar, harmonica or piano and composes new songs faster than he can remember them, there is no doubt that he is bursting at the seams with talent."

**Robert Shelton, New York Times, September 29, 1961**

Bob Dylan

CL 1779 / CS 8579 Stereo

WATCH FOR HIS NEW ALBUM TO BE RELEASED SOON

An advertisement for Dylan's first LP, from *Sing Out!* magazine, 1962.

# Looking Back

## D.A. Pennebaker interviewed by John Bauldie

*D.A.Pennebaker is one of the most celebrated cinema verite filmmakers. He filmed Bob Dylan in England in 1965 (for his own film,* Don't Look Back) *and in Europe in 1966 (for Bob Dylan's film,* Eat The Document). *The interview took place in New York City on July 15, 1986.*

*How did* Don't Look Back *all begin for you? What actually started it off?*

Well I'd been thinking about doing a film on music at the time because music was interesting. I had talked to somebody who knew the Stones – it was a kid who was kinda playing with them, whose mother was a film editor in London, still is, and so I thought of that and went over, but that didn't seem quite right. And then I thought of Baez – she was fairly well known – but that wasn't what seemed to me was interesting. I had a definite idea in my head, you see. But I didn't know about Dylan at all; I'd maybe heard his name, but I had no idea...

So I was thinking about it – had been for about a year and a half – and it got to the fall of 1964. And then Albert Grossman came in one day. I wasn't there, I was out having lunch or something, but Ricky Leacock, my partner, was there. And Albert came in and said, "I represent Bob Dylan. Is anybody here interested in making a film about him?" And Leacock said, "Who's Bob Dylan?" So Albert said, "Maybe I'd better come back again."

He and Dylan had approached us because Sara had worked with us at *Life*. She was working there for about a year and a half, so I knew Sara quite well. Then I came back, and Albert said, "My client's going to England; would you like to make a film about it?" I

44

said, "Sure." And he said "OK, I'll arrange for you to meet him." I don't think at that point that the question of money even came up. He assumed, I think, that we could somehow raise the money for the Dylan film. I figured we could too, so I was kind of astonished when we went to Columbia and said, "You guys interested in putting up any money?" and the guy there said, "Well, we got a couple of records of Dylan's that we're waiting to release – maybe I'll put you in touch with the guy who'll be in charge of that." And he sent me down to some guy, and I said, "Look, I'm not looking to make a lot of money out of this, but if I could get our expenses paid – just getting to England and back – we'll put up all the film and everything, as long as we can get that back ultimately. For $5,000 I'll give you half the film." They said, "No."

So I realised it was going to be a tough one to sell! And so I went to some friends of mine who were just beginning to set up *60 Minutes*, and a guy named Ike Kleineman said, "Well, I'll buy some footage from you – maybe $500-$600 worth of footage – if it's terrific footage." And I said, "Well, that's good." And so I *knew* that it wasn't going to be easy to sell. Then again, none of our films are easy to sell.

*So you paid the entire production costs?*

We put up all the money for the film. Albert didn't put up any money. He put up the tickets for Jones and Howard Alk to get over there, that's all, and they were basically friends of his, so I didn't figure that was too administrative – and so in the end we put up all the money for the film. The idea was that we would get reimbursed out of first moneys up to $100,000 – that was the deal. It was just written on a piece of paper, the bottom of a menu somewhere, it was a handshake deal. I don't think we ever had a formal contract between us. Dylan and I shook hands and that was it.

Later, I think that when Albert saw that the film was going to have some theatrical run – he hadn't ever envisaged this and anyway I think he had it in his head that Bob was going to make a film with Warners – Bob didn't want to make it, but there was a lot of money at stake – anyway, I remember that Albert had never really thought of my film as a real film, it seemed awfully home-movie-ish to him to have any kind of reality, but when he saw the poster he came in grudgingly and said, "That's a terrific poster. What are you gonna do?" I said, "Well, Albert, we're gonna release it because that's the understanding and we're partners on it. I can't afford to take a wash on it." And he said, "Well, I don't think you should release it. I think you should let me distribute it." And I said, "No, I can't do that." Albert, I think, felt we kinda squished him maybe on *Don't Look Back*.

*What do you think Dylan's motivation was?*

I don't know. And I am not sure that it's meaningful to try to second guess. My sense is that the reason that they let us make films – Jane Fonda, Kennedy, all of 'em – was that they figured that they'd find out something interesting by looking at the film. With Dylan there may have been that. He'd seen a couple of films that we'd done, so he knew a little that what we did was peculiar and different. I think that Dylan had a very parochial sense about his operation. He was going to do things totally differently from the way they'd been done; he was gonna revamp network schedules; he was gonna revamp movies; he was gonna make everything in a new way – without being quite sure how he'd do it. In many ways Dylan's very naive, extremely naive about things – amazingly so. In other ways he's an old seer or something – I mean he's not your normal type of person to deal with!

But I think that he thought that this was a way to find out about films and, basically, Dylan always counts a nickel, it was gonna be cheap – it wasn't gonna cost him anything! And I'm sure that Albert explained to him that the deal was for them to pick up some footage they could use for commercials abroad. Everybody – The Beatles, the Stones – they did these TV promo things free; that was standard, that's what you did on English TV at that time to sell a record. In fact, that whole thing with the cards was really done like a TV promo for "Subterranean Homesick Blues". The thing with the cards was Dylan's idea, and we shot three versions while we were in London – one in the park, one on a roof and one in the back alley right behind the Savoy hotel. I went there recently – they're still working on that goddam alley! It still has the same scaffolding! Anyway, in the one in the park we got arrested in the middle so you can see that the heavy hand of the law comes in just about the time he's doing one of the last cards...

*Did you keep the camera running?*

Oh yeah. We've got 'em all some place. Everyone helped in writing out those signs – Joan did some and Donovan did a lot of the signs. You know Donovan's a very good drawer? He turned out to be the artist, so everybody gave him the hard ones to do.

*So from the time you were approached in 1964 and you weren't really aware of Dylan, to the time that the trip was set up – let's say in April 1965 – presumably you encountered Dylan's music in the meantime?*

Albert sent me a couple of records, yeah.

*And what were your feelings about them?*

The songs really hit me. From then on I knew that by total chance I'd fallen right into the place that I should be. That happens maybe 10 per cent of the time in filmmaking. If you're not lucky, you shouldn't do it. You get used to knowing that you're in the right place and not wondering how you got there or why. And that's why you don't look for contracts or anything else, 'cos when you're in the right place, you have a tremendous amount of power – and everybody kind of realises that.

*The High Sheriff's Lady was recently in the newspapers. She still has the harmonica.*

That was hysterical. It's such a funny scene. I love it because it totally takes the curse off Dylan and the Science Student. There was a problem in that scene – it sort of blinks a little as if the lights were blinking. That was because the battery for the camera had run down and I had to wind the take-up reel by hand which pulled the film through the camera, and try to make sure that I did it at the right speed. You could do that with my old camera, but you'd have a hard time doing that with the new rigs. I couldn't believe that I'd shot it.

*I thought that Dylan was being kind to the Science Student.*

I did too. You know, everybody has different feelings about those things – him and the *Time* reporter. I knew who the *Time* reporter was – I have the story he sent back about that meeting and he was not at all vindictive towards Dylan. I thought that Dylan was pretty decent to him too.

*He's trying to teach him...*

Yeah, trying to tell him something that this guy had resisted learning his whole life long. I thought that Dylan was very patient with him, and took the curse off it by making the joke at the end.

And the final, incredible scene which to me is one of the perfect scenes that you fall on – the moment when you can't make a mistake, and you know you're right in the centre and you just shoot everything that moves, and you don't even think about why or how, you just shoot it, it's in your lap – going in the cab to the Albert Hall, when Fred starts talking about his "other" folksinger, Donovan, and Bob says, "How's he doing?" and then Fred does the trashing of Donovan. And Dylan never cracks. He just looks out the window.

Fantastic! It's just fantastic! Just one shot. You didn't have to edit anything; it told you everything. Those to me were really high moments of filmmaking in that kind of film. And they don't come every film – just once in a while.

*The scene with Albert dealing with Tito Burns – it's really looking deep into the workings of their operation.*

Neither of them think so! Albert did say that after a while he got tired of little girls coming up to him in clubs, telling him how gross he looked in that scene – he almost wished he hadn't done it; but Tito, he wrote me a letter and he thinks he's a movie star! "I'll be with Albert in about 10 minutes" – you couldn't get people to *act* funnier.

*In the whole film I can only recall one time when Dylan glances at the camera...*

When they're throwing the hotel guy out of the room?

*Yeah. Telling the assistant to go to his fop manager.*

The fop manager! Actually, he does one other; it's when he's playing with Alan Price – when he asks Alan if he's playing with The Animals any more, and he says, "No, it happens," and then Dylan starts to chord in those blues. And then he looked at me like he was kinda pissed that I was filming. But I didn't give a shit. It was one of those things where we were looking right in the eye.

And then he looked away. But you can see that mean look he sometimes gives.

*The clip of Dylan in Greenwood, Mississippi in 1963 that you spliced into* Don't Look Back, *did you use that in its entirety?*

Yeah. The guy who sent it to me, Ed Emshwiller, didn't know what to do with it. I guess Albert had told them that they couldn't use it in their film – they did a film on folk called *Streets Of Greenwood*, or something like that – it was done by a couple of guys, but Emshwiller was the cameraman. And Ed Emshwiller to this day uses a wind-up Bolex – that's his camera! So he was down there shooting Dylan singing with a wind-up Bolex, and they figured there was no way to sync it up, though they did have a track of it. So they said, "Pennebaker, you might as well have it," 'cos they didn't know what to do with it. So they sent it over to me, and I thought, "God, what am I gonna do with this?" Mississippi was certainly nothing to do with my film. So I stuck it over my editing bench. It sat there, and I put the whole thing out of my mind.

I wasn't even working on *Don't Look Back*, but there was this friend of Howard's and Dylan's who was working for me then, briefly, from Chicago. His name was Quinn. And he kept saying, "You're too busy; you're not going to edit that film. Let me edit it." I said, "No, I'll get to it." So it sat there for a long time. And then one day I decided to do it. So I settled down with just a viewer, and I got my first flush of enthusiasm when the guy says, "How did it all begin?" And I stopped. And it started me thinking. And then I saw that thing sitting on the shelf, so I decided I might as well look at it. Now when you use a viewer to edit, you have the viewer and you have a synchroniser sitting here with a reader on the synchroniser, and they're roughly 22 frames apart. So you never let anything go out, because once it gets out you gotta thread up – and it's hard to do that. So I had these pieces of film from the last scene still sticking out – "How did it all begin, Bob?" – and I just spliced the Greenwood film on, just to look at it, not as part of the film, 'cos that's the way you look at stuff. And when I looked at it, I thought, "Holy shit!" And I never took it out of the film.

*That's one of my favourite parts of the film – not just the cut, but when the guy from the African service comes out with this amazingly demanding question – "How do you see the art of the folk-song in contemporary society?" – and asks for Dylan's approval. And Dylan nods! But of course, we never get to hear an answer to that question.*

Well, he could never answer. He never did answer. You know he's not going to answer that question. I like the idea that he can't answer. He just sits there with that funny look while the guy is going on and on about his friend! I love that.

I had another thing that was funny that I wanted to use but didn't. It was too easy. This guy seemed to be fair game. The guy came in and played Dylan some easy listening music tracks of half a dozen of Dylan's songs – a string orchestra! And Bob had to sit there and listen. He didn't dare catch my eye. And this guy was so excited to be playing this stuff for him, but it was driving Dylan crazy to have to listen to it for five minutes.

*The tension that was in the film about expecting Donovan, that was for real?*

Oh yeah. We didn't know who Donovan was. Well, it was kind of a joke that Dylan worked up, because Albert was saying, "We're gonna have The Beatles over – then there's this new folk singer, Donovan!" Anyway, Donovan was gonna come around one night, for supper or something, and so we were waiting – Bob and I and Neuwirth. I said, "I'll shoot it," but Bob said, "No, you can't shoot it." But we all had to put masks on – Hallowe'en masks.

And Donovan knocked on the door, and there were the three of us sitting at the table. And he came in, you know – he was a kid – and there were these three guys, and he didn't know which one was Dylan. And he was laughing. And Dylan kinda broke up a little bit, 'cos he did like him. I used to catch Dylan listening to "Catch The Wind" – there was one little phrase in there that Dylan really got off on – so he liked Donovan before he even saw him. He liked the idea of Donovan. So he laughed and told Donovan to sit down. Well, Donovan was very excited and decided to play something for him. Dylan said he liked "Catch The Wind", but Donovan said, "I've written a new song I wanna play for you." So he played a song called "My Darling Tangerine Eyes". And it was to the tune of "Mr Tambourine Man"! And Dylan was sitting there with this funny look on his face, listening to "Mr Tambourine Man" with these really weird words, and about halfway through the second verse, Donovan realises that Dylan is cracking up – and Neuwirth and I were fighting it back, it was so crazy, trying to keep a straight face.

Then Dylan says, "Well...you know...that *tune!*" Dylan said, "I have to admit that I haven't written *all* the tunes that I'm credited with, but that happens to be one that I *did* write!" And Donovan says, "Oh. I didn't know! I thought it was an old folk tune!" Well, Dylan says, "Go on – keep playing!" and Donovan says, "Oh no. I won't play any more." I'm sure he never played the song again.

*Can I ask you about the Joan Baez relationship at this time? There have been certain statements by Baez herself that she felt very alienated, treated very badly by Dylan at that time, and yet in the film – even for example in the scene where Dylan and Neuwirth are joshing with her about having the see-thru blouse you don't even wanna – there doesn't really seem to be any malice, or....*

Well you've got to understand a peculiar situation around royal entourages, palaces, courts in general, politics, and that is that you can be number four or five, but if you're used to being one or two it's a big jolt – and that's kind of what that was about. There were other people in Dylan's life – there was Sara – and Baez kind of knew it. She was having a hard time I think at that moment in her life. I don't know why, but emotionally she was feeling very roughed up by life. To be honest, I don't think that Dylan had invited her to be there, but Albert had said, "Come along," and so she came, knowing that that's not the same thing as being demanded. And I think that that hurt her, y'know, that she was no longer Queen. She was dragging Dylan, who didn't want to be a part of that scene any more, and I think that she knew that; but at the same time she wanted to be there because... well, she loved him. And that music was exciting to her – I don't mean what he was doing, but what he was about to do. She could smell it coming. He was breaking away from all the old stuff and she wanted to too; she wanted to do a rock'n'roll album very badly. I was very sympathetic to her. I really liked her a lot. After that I was going to do a film with her, but there was nobody interested.

*I love the scene in the hotel room with Joan Baez when Dylan sings the Hank Williams songs. Can you remember how long he was singing for that night?*

Oh he sang a lot. I have a lot more film of that. They did one marvellous one, Joan and he, that I was going to use, but it was a little too long: "Good news travels slow, but bad news travels like wildfire". Do you know that song? It's a great song, and they sang it together.

*You don't happen to have that here do you?*

Probably. Dylan's looked at it, and it's all piled up, but I'd be happy to show it to you if we can get permission. "Brown-Eyed Girl" I kinda liked too.

*"Brown-Eyed Girl"? Van Morrison's song?*

I don't think so – I'm not sure. He only sang a bit of it at a mic check. He often sang songs that you never knew about – and never heard again – bits of songs sometimes – that were so fantastic they could make you cry.

*You were talking about Albert Grossman before...*

Albert was always a good friend of mine, I always considered him a good friend. I used to talk to him up 'til a few months ago, before he died. So I never had the sense that Albert was in any way an enemy, which I knew had become the situation subsequently with Albert and Bob – that they were really enemies. Which is too bad, because I think Albert was one of the few people that saw Dylan's worth very early on, and played it absolutely without equivocation or any kind of compromise. He refused to let him go on any rinkydink TV shows, refused to let Columbia do bullshit things with him – which they did with a lot of other people, you know. And Dylan, I think, in his early stages, required that kind of handling – 'cos Dylan himself would go off at spurious tangents. One week he'd do one thing and another week he'd do something else – and maybe in the end he would have prevailed. I mean, he came close to not prevailing, we kinda know that, but in the end he pulled himself together and did what very few people in his position have done, which was to really survive. I don't mean just to be hanging around...

And I think that of all the things, that's the most interesting thing about Dylan – that health prevails as well as whatever – genius, talent, whatever else you ascribe to him – the fact that his intelligence made him survive is really interesting. And I think Albert had something to do with that. When Albert died, I wrote Bob a letter and I said a lot of bad things have gone down between them, but I knew that basically Albert was extremely devoted to him and loved him – and I knew that Bob loved Albert; so it was really kind of sad that it had come to that. But... these things happen.

*Can you say something more about Sara? She's someone who's hardly spoken of or written about at all.*

Well, she was always a very private person. Actually she and Sally Grossman were friends – they roomed together down in the Village. Sara had been a bunny for a while and was about with Victor Lownes – she was Sara Lowndes – and Dylan kind of snitched her away from him. She was really a beautiful woman... fantastic looking – and she had a very strange personality, a kind that went for health food and mysterious life... it seemed to me at the time a very ersatz philosophy – what mattered and what didn't. She seemed on the surface to have that, but underneath she was clearly a very interesting person. For a long time she worked up at the magazine, for our unit – we were kind of a secret unit working on *Life*. I had a studio downtown and she took charge of the uptown office; so she and I were really managing the whole operation in 1963. Then she quit, she got pregnant, and had a child – although I can't remember whether she was still there when I quit in July 1964. I would have hired her myself, 'cos she wanted to get away from *Life* too, but I really couldn't afford it. And then she went off – went into some sort of mysterious phase in the Village – and I saw her off and on. Then I didn't see her a lot for a long time. But she was one of the first people I showed *Don't Look Back* to. I haven't seen her for a long time.

*You said before that Dylan himself was looking at the film you have?*

Yeah, he went through a lot of stuff, and he did make up some kind of a tape – I never saw the thing – recently. He would come in around nine or 10 at night and work through 'til maybe three in the morning – he likes to work at night. And he picked out some pieces – one of the things that interested him was one of the songs he sang in 1965, "To Ramona", and we noticed a reference to it in *The Telegraph*! Somebody caught it! That was amazing. I didn't think anybody would notice.

*It was shown on the "20/20" show.*

Yeah. It was not from *Don't Look Back*. Well, he did that. He liked that. He came in and he was looking at all the film he could. And he was saying things like, "How do you get that wonderful effect of it all being shot from one point of view?" So I said, "That's easy. You can only afford to hire one camera."

## The Science Student

*After his roasting in the dressing room in Newcastle, 1965, Terry Ellis, the "science student", went on to pursue a career in rock'n'roll. He subsequently founded Chrysalis Records and is currently Chairman of the British Phonographic Industries.*

"I wasn't meant to interview Dylan at the time because he'd said he wasn't going to do any more interviews. At the time, Dylan was chewing journalists up and spitting them out, so I wasn't even that keen to talk to him.

Funnily enough, I didn't actually have tickets for the gig, but because I used to go and interview bands at the Newcastle City Hall quite regularly for the student magazine I wrote for, I knew the people on the door, so I just said to them, I've come to interview Dylan, and they said, Well you can come in but he's not doing interviews.

Once I was in, I just went into the hall, and I was hanging about there waiting for the gig to start and I suddenly got a tap on the shoulder and one of Dylan's roadies came up to me and said, He'll see ya now. Well, as you can imagine, I browned my trousers. I didn't know what to do. I meekly followed him and in I went, terrified.

Dylan was stalking around the dressing room, strumming his guitar. He was very slight but he gives off a powerful kind of aura. I remember he had a wicked glint in his eye – I couldn't tell you if it was chemically induced or not, but I just remember feeling, at this point, like a lamb going to the slaughter.

In retrospect, I don't think he was actually being cruel to me, he was being quite pleasant, but in his own caustic way. Dylan was just playing a game with me. I was just a kid and they were having a bit of a giggle. He gave me a hard time, but in a way I put up a bit of a fight..."

*(Interview: Adrian Deevoy)*

# Newport '65

## Joe Boyd interviewed by Jonathan Morley

*Joe Boyd, now head of his own Hannibal Records in London, was the production manager at the Newport Folk Festival in 1965, when Dylan played his infamous electric set with the Paul Butterfield Blues Band. Did they really boo...? Interview: London, August 31, 1988.*

*Bob Dylan....*

...I have no real significance in the history of Bob Dylan's career whatsoever but, for people who are interested in Dylan, I did encounter him in a number of different and sometimes interesting circumstances between 1962 and 1965. I think that to understand the context of the first contact I had with him, I should mention the different schools of rivalries in the American folk scene at the time. It was very much a Boston versus New York split, and basically the Boston school was much more ethnic-oriented: people there were interested in the authenticity of the re-creation of old blues, country music, bluegrass... Eric Von Schmidt for example, all the people who became the Kweskin Jug Band, Geoff Muldaur, Jim Kweskin, Bill Keith, Jim Rooney.

In New York it was very political. By contrast, New York was very much following in or under the influence of the strength of the popularity of Pete Seeger and The Weavers during the '50s and the context in which Leadbelly and Big Bill Broonzy and Woody Guthrie and Cisco Houston had been brought into the scene.

To reduce it to a rather cartoonish level, at its most blatant, the difference was that the Boston people wanted to sing and sound exactly like a Mississippi plantation negro of 1930, whereas the point in New York was to sing that same song in exactly the same style in which you would sing a Spanish Civil War song and a cowboy song, to emphasise the brotherhood of all men, and to make it very easy for the masses to sing along.

That was the Pete Seeger philosophy in a way, and so there was a tremendous suspicion of New York in Boston and vice versa. The Boston coffeehouses were not overly receptive to New York people, they were very sceptical about them. Boston felt itself to be the centre of things, and there started to be noise about this kid from New York, Bob Dylan.

*Where were you at this time?*

I was going to Harvard and hanging out at the Club 47, which was the local Boston coffeehouse. I was very much in the Boston school. Eric Von Schmidt had told me that he had thought that Bob Dylan was really talented, and somebody played me his first album. I heard "Baby Let Me Follow You Down", which he learned off Eric Von Schmidt, and I was very disappointed. I felt it was a very superficial version of it and not a patch on Von Schmidt's. A few weeks after this album came out I was at a party in Harvard Square and there was a rumour that Dylan was in town, and people were saying he was coming up for the weekend.

He already had a charisma of some kind among the singers; he was known to be somebody that everybody was talking about in New York, and I think Joan Baez, who was still very much the Queen of Harvard Square, kept talking about Dylan and how keen she was on him. In fact, I think the reason for Dylan's visit was Joan Baez's concert at Symphony Hall, which was a big event. I think she had invited him to come up and do a song with her on stage, and I think he obviously wanted to do it because it was a good splash for him.

So I went to this party, wandering around, talking, and then going into a back room; and there were about eight people seated on the floor and on the bed was Dylan singing "A Hard Rain's A-Gonna Fall". I was absolutely overwhelmed. It was just an incredibly powerful performance and any scepticism which I'd had, based on my scant exposure, was just blown out of the window and I became a very strong fan. The next night I went over to Eric Von Schmidt's with a couple of friends, and he said that Dylan was coming over. And Dylan eventually came over and we were introduced. Then he said he had to go down to Symphony Hall.

*What were your impressions when you met him?*

He was all the cliches that you hear about him; he was medium-size and wiry, and rather sarcastic and funny and a bit closed. I mean, he wasn't an overly friendly guy to people he didn't know; he wasn't a warm, open-hearted sort of guy. Anyway, we all went down to Symphony Hall, and it was getting towards the end of Joan Baez's concert and I think she was a bit peeved because he was late, but he just showed up and we all went backstage and he waved at her from the wings and she invited him to come out on stage and they sang – I can't remember what – "Blowin' In The Wind" or "Masters Of War", something like that, as a duet. And I think he sang something on his own and everybody went nuts.

I saw him a few other times on trips to Boston subsequently, but really he was very much a New York phenomenon, and not somebody that I had particularly close contact with. But I did have one very amusing incident when I went back to Boston after I finished college, which was a couple of years later. It was the summer of '64 and I ran into a girl that I had known off and on during the time and I'd always quite fancied but never really got to know particularly well, and she and I had coffee and spent the afternoon together, and she had to go to work as a waitress in some bar. I think there was a buzz at the time that Dylan was in town, doing a big concert of his own at Symphony Hall, and she talked about how some friends had promised to take her along to the concert, late, so she could see the end of it and get backstage, but she had to work in the evening up until that time.

Now I didn't really have a place to stay and so she said, "Stay with me"; and I'd gone to her house, dropped my bag in the bedroom, and she'd said, "Look, I'll be home by 12 so come by any time after 12" – because I was going to see some friends, do something different. I was quite pleased by this turn of events, strutting around all evening with this inner glow, knowing that treats were in store, so around 12.30 I roll up at her place; there's a key under her mat and there's a note with a big sign – "JOE" – and the door to her bedroom was closed, and there's a pillow and sheet on the couch. And the note says, "I'm afraid there's been a change of plan. You'll never guess who's here!!!!!" So I went to sleep on the couch, and in the morning I had breakfast with her and Dylan. She told me later, "I was looking forward to it, Joe, but, you know, can't turn down that opportunity!"

I went to Chicago at the beginning of 1965 and helped Elektra get the Paul Butterfield Band signed – I recommended Mike Bloomfield as an additional guitar player because Paul Rothchild felt that Elvin Bishop wasn't a strong enough player. So I knew all those guys. My basic job was working for George Wein, a job I got lined up at college, as tour manager in Europe and production manager at the Newport Jazz and Folk Festivals. I had been in Europe for the '64 Folk Festival, but I had been at the '62 and '63 Festivals and I'd always felt that the sound was very bad – it was just amateurish the way it was done. So when it came to the '65 Festival I said, "OK, if I'm gonna be in charge of the stage, we're gonna have good sound this year." And I went to the Board – in effect, the Festival was run by a Board of Directors, a non-profit organisation which included Peter Yarrow (of Peter, Paul & Mary), Theodore Bikel, Alan Lomax, Ralph Rinzler, Ronnie Gilbert and a few other people like that from the folky establishment. So I went to the Board and said, "Look, you've got to hire somebody who really knows how to mix sound to do the sound for the festival." I recommended that they hire Paul Rothchild, who was a well-known folk musician producer at the time – he produced the Butterfield Band and eventually The Doors and Janis Joplin. He was a friend of mine. He said he'd love to do it.

So, we met and agreed that every single performer who went on the main stage would have a sound rehearsal, which had never been done before, so we were getting people up at 10 o'clock in the morning and dragging them out there. We had a sound rehearsal for the Texas Penitentiary Chain Gang Prisoners Singing Team, who sang when they chopped down a tree on stage! We did it all before the place opened and then between the afternoon session and the evening session we had another time when we did soundchecks. I was out there almost 18 hours a day shuttling people back and forth.

The events of Newport 1965 have been fairly well documented elsewhere. In '64 Dylan had been the King of Newport. I wasn't there, but I know from all that happened that it was the apex of the dream of the New York folk scene. Dylan was the answer to their prayers, in a way. Everything they had struggled through, the McCarthy period, they'd all struggled through the '50s, all that sort of thing, and finally here was a guy who had taken up the mantle of Woody Guthrie, who was singing protest songs, politically aware songs, and getting them to Number 1 in the charts. And young, white, middle-class kids by the thousands were going south in the summer to register as voters in Mississippi, were protesting against the Vietnam war, were protesting against segregation... It was a very, very exciting time, and Dylan was the focus. It was wonderful. It was a terrific, exciting thing to see, and to be around, and to be part of, and Dylan was the vortex of it.

Now the 1965 Folk Festival came at a time when on the radio you were hearing "I Got You Babe" by Sonny & Cher, which was obviously a Dylan rip-off, "Like A Rolling Stone", The Byrds singing "Mr Tambourine Man". There was something happening! Things were changing. Seeger and the rest of those people would have liked to have bottled the lightning of 1964, preserved it, and kept it just that way. But it wasn't staying that way. By this time all those parochial old folky distinctions and jealousies had been blown away by Dylan and The Beatles in the summer of optimism and expansion of the horizons. Suddenly it was veering away from "Blowin' In The Wind". What was "Mr Tambourine Man" about? That wasn't politics! That was something else. That was WEIRD! There was a tremendous anticipation at Newport about Dylan.

*About what he was going to do?*

Well, no – "Is he here yet? Has he arrived?" And instead of this blue-jeaned, work-shirted guy who'd arrived in '64 to be the Pied Piper, he arrived rather secretively; he was staying in a luxurious hotel just on the outside of town and he arrived with Bob Neuwirth and Al Kooper – that was the entourage, Neuwirth, Kooper and Dylan, and they were all wearing puff-sleeved duelling shirts – one of them was polka dot – and they were wearing not blue jeans, but some kinda I-can't-remember-what sorta trousers. And they wore sunglasses. The whole image was very, very different. They were very clannish, very secretive.

All the performers did what they called workshops during the day, just small performances on the small stages around the grounds, and Dylan, of course, was scheduled to sing in the Songwriters' Workshop, and unlike the year before and previous years when there was always a good spread of attendance between workshops which were going on at the same time in different parts of the grounds – Blues, Bluegrass Banjo-picking, Country Fiddle – this year the crowd around the Songwriters' Workshop was so immense that it was swamping the other workshops. People were complaining – "Turn up the Dylan one because we're getting bleed from the Banjo-picking one on the other side!" This was very much against the spirit of what the festival was supposed to be about, and the officials were starting to get tense.

In fact, they were tense to begin with because things were happening in the air that summer that they didn't understand and that they weren't prepared for. They were very, very paranoid about people smoking marijuana, for example. They were nervous about the WHOLE THING. And Dylan's appearance, his manner, the songs he sang at the workshop, everything added to their disquiet.

Albert Grossman, Dylan's manager, became a focus of hostility for a lot of them. He'd never been popular amongst these people. He'd always been seen as one of the money changers at the gates of the temple and not a priest, y'know, and Grossman was arrogant, particularly with Dylan now being so big. Grossman was being very cool, but Grossman's way of being cool got up people's noses.

The flashpoint came at the Blues workshop at the end of the day. There had been a lot of pressure from Peter Yarrow on adding the Paul Butterfield Band to the line-up of the festival – he really put a lot of pressure on the other members of the Board to get the invitation, and Lomax was really against it – against Butterfield, against white boys doing the blues really. I'm sure the people that were nervous and theoretically in charge of the festival couldn't have analysed what they objected to, but they knew that it smelled wrong; they knew that there was something up that they didn't want – it was hostile to their interests. The so-called revolution which they started was just about to veer off-course, and this was deeply disturbing because they had just gotten there – just gotten to their life's dream, and suddenly it was all disappearing in a cloud of marijuana smoke and weird lyrics!

The Butterfield Band in their coolness and their hipness and their white-boys-wearing-dark-glasses kind of Chicago look were obviously a part of this trend, and they didn't like it – and Lomax was forced to introduce the Butterfield Band at the Blues workshop, and he gave them an introduction which was very condescending. Well, as the group started to take the stage, Lomax came off stage to be confronted by Grossman who, basically, said unkind words about the introduction that Lomax had just given. I don't know what was said, something like, "That was a real chickenshit introduction, Alan" and Lomax just pushed him aside and said, "Out of my way, Grossman", and the next thing you know is these two men, both rather oversized, were rolling around in the dirt throwing punches. They had to be pulled apart.

Lomax then called an emergency meeting of the Board of the festival that night, about 6.30 or 7 o'clock, before the evening concert, and then... I wasn't there, but George Wein gave me the gist of what had been said, which was, basically, that they wanted Grossman banned from the grounds. They felt that he was giving drugs to the performers, he'd hit Alan Lomax, he was a very bad influence etc etc, and the Board – I don't know who voted how – but the Board actually voted in favour of banning Grossman from the grounds of the festival!

George Wein, who was a non-voting advisor to the Board, had to step in and say, "Look, I don't have a vote, it's up to you, but I can tell you right now that if you do bar Grossman you have to prepare yourselves for the walk out of Bob Dylan, Peter, Paul & Mary and Buffy St Marie," and that he, George Wein, did not want to have to be the one to give them their money back and like it or not, contrary to the spirit of the festival or not, the fact was that a good 40 to 50 per cent of the people out there were coming to see Peter, Paul & Mary and Dylan, and if they weren't on the bill those people were going to feel very aggrieved, and he felt that the decision should be reconsidered. So the Board reconsidered and dropped the action against Grossman. But there was, obviously, a tremendous simmering of feeling.

On Sunday afternoon, by the time the concert had finished and before the start of the Butterfield Band set that evening – they'd been pushed back because they couldn't play in the afternoon because their amps were wet – we had an hour and a half or two hours to do our soundchecks. Now we had known that Dylan was going to do something with more than just himself – there'd been rumours of secret rehearsals in this hotel that he was staying at – and that he was going to need a soundcheck...

*Dylan wanted the soundcheck?*

Oh yeah, he wanted the soundcheck. And Grossman. I went to Grossman the day before and I said, "You guys, we want you to have a soundcheck – do you want a soundcheck?" And he'd said, "You bet we want a soundcheck." Anyway, so on came Dylan with the Butterfield Band and Al Kooper on keyboards. We set up the stage the way they wanted it set up – it had to be set up anyway for Butterfield's first set – and they started playing. Obviously, this was great! We all knew that this was significant. It was really exciting stuff, there was no question about it.

*What was it?*

Well, it was the three songs. I said, "How many songs are you going to do?" And they – Butterfield, Bloomfield and Dylan – looked at each other and said, "Well, we only know three, so that's what we're gonna do." And I said, "Well, you know, they're going to want a little more than that." And Dylan said, "It's all we got an' it's all we're gonna do." He was being very sort of moody about it.

Well, the concert took place, and Dylan wasn't even on at the end of the concert, he was on in the middle. He was on one act before the interval, at around 9.15. So out comes Dylan, and I'm out there on the stage before he comes out, setting up all the amps to exactly the right levels, and Rothchild's out at the mixing board, right in the middle of the audience, where it would be today at a concert, getting everything cranked up. And when that first note of "Maggie's Farm" hit... I mean, by today's standards it's not very loud, but by those standards of the day it was the loudest thing that anybody had ever heard.

The volume. That was the thing, the volume. It wasn't just the music, it wasn't just the fact that he came out and played with an electric band, it was the fact... and this, I suppose, is what this whole thing is leading up to... the only significance that I can claim in this whole saga is just the fact that care was taken to get Paul Rothchild to mix the sound. As a result, you didn't have some square sound guy fumbling around, you had powerfully, ballsy-mixed, expertly done rock'n'roll.

*So you enjoyed it?*

Yeah! When they came out the first hit of the guitar was like... PPPAARRR! A wall of sound, you know, hitting the audience with tremendous power. It really knocked people back on their seats. As soon as I had gotten the stage set, I ran around to the press enclosure which was the front section, and stood sort of at the door and watched at the side of the stage and I thought, "This is great!" I was lapping it all up.

Then somebody pulled at my elbow and said, "You'd better go backstage, they want to talk to you." So I went backstage and there I was confronted by Seeger and Lomax and, I think, Theodore Bikel or somebody, saying, "It's too loud! You've got to turn it down! It's far too loud! We can't have it like this! It's just *unbearably* loud!" And they were really upset. Very, very upset. I said, "Well, I don't control the sound, the sound is out there in the middle of the audience." And so Lomax said, "How do you get there? Tell me how to get there, I'll go out there!" I said, "Well, Alan, you walk right to the back – it's only about half a mile – and then you walk around to the centre thing, show your badge, and just come down the centre aisle." And he said, "There must be a quicker way." So I said, "Well, you can climb over the fence" – I was looking at his girth, you know – and he said, "Now look, you go out there, you can get there, I know you know how to get there. Go out there and tell them that the Board *orders* them to turn the sound down!"

I said, "OK." So I went out – there was a place where anyone could climb on top of a box and get over the fence from backstage. By this time I think it was the beginning of the second number, and there were Grossman and Neuwirth and Yarrow and Rothchild all sitting at the sound desk, grinning, very very pleased with themselves – and meanwhile the audience was going nuts.

*Nuts in what way?*

Well, you couldn't tell. I would've said it was about half-and-half. There were arguments between people sitting next to each other! Some were booing, some were cheering. It was very very hard to tell. There was a ROAR of noise. I mean, it was definitely shocking. I relayed Lomax's message and Peter Yarrow said, "Tell Alan Lomax..." and he extended his middle finger. And I said, "C'mon Peter, gimme a break!" He said, "Well, just tell Alan that the Board of the festival are adequately represented on the sound console and that we have things fully under control and we think that the sound is at the correct level."

So I went back, climbed over the fence, and by this time all I could see of Pete Seeger was the back of him disappearing down the road past the car park. I was confronted by Lomax and Bikel again, frothing at the mouth, and I relayed Yarrow's message and they just cursed and gnashed their teeth. By this time the thing was almost over. Yarrow followed me back – I think he'd had a conversation with Dylan earlier in which he'd said, "You can't just do three numbers. You've got to come on and do some acoustic stuff afterwards." 'Cos Dylan had been scheduled for 40 minutes, certainly half an hour. People had not come all that way to see 20 minutes of Bob Dylan, or 15... So Yarrow was all poised to go up on stage, and suddenly they'd finished.

There was a HUGE roar from the crowd...you know, "More!!" and "Boo!!" sound very similar if you have a whole crowd going "More!!" and "Boo!!" – you couldn't really tell what was happening. I think it was evenly divided between approbation and condemnation from the crowd. Well, this roar went on for quite some time and Yarrow then went on stage and rather embarrassingly began to do his impression of a sort of Las Vegas compere – "C'mon folks, let's hear it for Bob Dylan, see if we can get him back out here!" No Bob Dylan. Bob Dylan was hiding in a tent. Grossman didn't want to get involved. He wasn't going to bully Dylan about it. Anyway, finally Dylan stumbled back out on stage with an acoustic guitar and he went into "Mr Tambourine Man".

He did two songs – applause and approval – and then right after him were this amazing group of black gospel singers from the sea islands off South Carolina, the Moving Star Singers, who were really magnificent, and then there was the interval. After the interval for some reason the scheduling misfired and there was a parade of every washed-up, boring, old, folky, left-wing fart you could imagine, leading up to Peter, Paul & Mary in the final thing – Ronnie Gilbert, Oscar Brand, even Josh White, who was much beyond his powers at that point, Theodore Bikel – they all went on, one after another. You know, it was like an object lesson in what was going on here. Like, you guys are all washed up. This is all finished...

The thing I cherish about that evening was... there are a lot of occasions when you can look back and say, "Well, after that night things were never the same." But it's very rare that you're in a moment where you know it at the time, where you know as it's happening – and this was such an event. You knew, as it was happening, that paths were parting.

# Dylan and Warhol

## Gerard Malanga interviewed by John Bauldie

*Gerard Malanga was a central figure in Andy Warhol's Factory scene in the mid '60s. Working alongside Warhol in the painter's most creative days, Gerard was responsible for producing many of the famous silkscreens, one of which – the large Silver Elvis painting – was to play its own part in the Dylan-Warhol story. A poet, a painter, and later a dancer with the Exploding Plastic Inevitable and The Velvet Underground, Gerard was present when Andy Warhol made his "15 minutes of fame" quip, and was at The Factory when Bob Dylan and his friends called on Andy Warhol in 1965.*

*Had you met Bob before the visit to The Factory?*

Yes I did. Dylan had invited Andy and Edie and myself to see a concert he was giving somewhere upstate, in a famous rock'n'roll theatre, and we did all go to that concert. It was one of those transitional concerts – a little bit acoustic, a bit electric. Barbara Rubin had something to do with it all, as well.

*Barbara Rubin was very much an instigating factor in bringing Dylan and Andy together...*

Oh very much so. Barbara was the one who eventually got Dylan to come to The Factory. In fact, he had visited The Factory once already, when Andy wasn't there. Dylan and Brian Jones both showed up at The Factory one evening with Barbara, and I was there – they knew I was gonna be there – and we just sort of hung out. I may have thrown a reel of a movie on the screen, I don't remember, but we were there for a while and we may even have

67

gone out somewhere to a restaurant or a club or something afterwards.

*Dylan and Brian Jones is an interesting pairing – how were the two of them together?*

Well, Dylan was top honcho and Brian was like...not subservient, but slightly on a lower rung than Dylan. Dylan was the star in a sense. "Like A Rolling Stone" had come out and so Dylan was kinda like the top man to contend with.

*OK, so when the famous visit of Bob Dylan and his entourage to The Factory occurred, was it all sort of stage-managed by Barbara Rubin, the groupie who brought megastars together?*

No, not really. It was a very freewheeling, almost casual kind of scene. It was funny because the groups kind of split off – Dylan's group of people that included Bobby Neuwirth and other people that had come with him, a film crew as well, and then there were the people around Andy. And Barbara and I were sort of between the two in a sense; we were the bridges.

*At the time Andy must have been interested in what Dylan was doing, and certainly Dylan was interested in Andy's work...*

I don't know if Dylan was interested in Andy's work that much. I think he kind of frowned upon it to tell you the truth. Dylan represented a certain milieu that was almost the antithesis of Andy's milieu in the sense of you had the heterosexual grouping and you had the so-called homosexual grouping – that doesn't mean that we were all homosexuals, but it was the kind of aura that was cast upon each of these two groups. And Dylan's group obviously didn't take Andy that seriously, you know. They were out to walk all over Andy and walk away with something. And they did. Dylan walked away with a very expensive Elvis Presley painting.

*Was Edie Sedgwick around at the time?*

Yes. Edie was attracted to Dylan. Edie took an interest in Dylan, Dylan took an interest in Edie. Chuck Wein, who was Edie's sidekick, was kind of cultivating the relationship to get the fire going between them.

*Can I throw a couple of quotes at you? The first is from Jean Stein's* Edie *biography and talks of "Edie's leaving Andy for Dylan".*

Well, in a way she did, but it wasn't like she left Andy, her boyfriend, for Dylan, her new boyfriend. It wasn't anything like that. She was a very pretty girl and had quite a style about her, but ultimately she did not end up with Dylan. She basically had no talent. She was under the illusion that she was going to sing with Bob on a record, but Edie had no voice whatsoever – she couldn't sing. She was just looking for a different kind of excitement. Her scene with Andy was just coming to an end – Andy had no money to give her. Well, maybe Andy could have given her money, but the reason that he didn't pay her at that time with regard to her being in his films was that he didn't want to set a precedent. And so she walked off, thinking that she had better horizons ahead of her, with Bobby Neuwirth egging her on – he being the main connection between her and Dylan. And then, of course, the Dylan thing never came to pass, so she ended up being Bobby Neuwirth's girlfriend.

*And another quote, from Andy himself: "I missed having her around. I told myself it was probably a good thing that Dylan was taking care of her now, because maybe he knew how to do it better than we had."*

Hahahahahaha!

*What does that mean?*

Hahaha! God, that sounds so intelligent on Andy's part! Hmmm. It's kind of a patronising, backhanded statement to make.

*It implies that Andy had been "taking care of her"...*

Yeah. He really wasn't. It wasn't like Andy was paying her rent.

*What about the situation with Edie and drugs?*

This is a terrible thing. When that Edie Sedgwick biography came out, Andy just flipped out. He was really pissed, because the entire time that Edie was connected to the Warhol scene, Edie was not doing hard drugs and Andy didn't do hard drugs. The closest thing that Andy was doing, and Edie was doing the same, was popping Obitrol, which was a prescription diet pill. It was after Edie left Andy and got involved with Dylan and then she started being passed around from hand to hand so to speak, that she got involved with heavy drugs. It was not something that Andy created. Then again, it's probably not true that the Dylan group were responsible for Edie's demise...

*So, getting back to the visit to The Factory, what's the story of Dylan's screen test? Did that take place immediately he arrived?*

Well, maybe in the first 15 or 20 minutes.

*I read that it was "a 15-minute study in stillness and silence".*

No, it was three minutes of stillness and silence, 100 feet of film. He was smoking a cigarette. It was shot on a Bolex and Dylan had to look in the camera, wearing his sunglasses.

*What happened to that film?*

It's in the archive. The films are being catalogued by the Museum of Modern Art. I have a colour reel also, besides the black-and-white, of Dylan that I shot the same day. It's notebook footage. I could do a number of things with it – I could make stills and have a show of movie stills or any kind of weird thing. But that stuff I'm not going to show right now. It's not stuff I'm ready to deal with.

*And the silver Elvis painting – that was Dylan's "payment" for sitting for the screen test?*

Well, Dylan had said he wanted the painting and Andy kind of flickered, but he gave it to him, as an enticement perhaps, hoping that Dylan might be in one of his movies, perhaps opposite Edie. Of course, that never really came to be. Knowing Andy, and how possessive he was with his art, I suspect it must have really irked him to give away the painting.

*You're implying that for Dylan the Elvis painting was a sort of prize that he carried off...*

Well, in a way. I actually saw Bobby and Bob tie the painting on top of the roof of their station wagon. I watched them rope it on – it had a piece of plastic over it – and it was funny to see it go like that. Dylan may have been the only one ever to pull that one off. Andy didn't really expect that Dylan was gonna be so... what's the word?... he was very forward in his manner. Dylan pulled the number first, but in agreeing to give it to him, Andy was hoping that this was the way to get Dylan to be in an Andy Warhol movie. But the closest thing Dylan came to that was the screen test.

# Paul McCartney

"1966...the main thing is that people were getting high, that's the main thing. It was the shift from drink to pot in fact – that's really all it was. There'd always been pills on the fringe of it, but then that was really what it was, so it became a bit more of a beatnik scene. And Dylan was a big influence. He was coming out of the New York poetry thing and we were crossing over into each other and you'd meet him and his thing would be, Where's the joint, man? And we'd go, What's that then? What do you mean?

I remember going to see Dylan when he was at the Mayfair Hotel and we went to pay homage and he'd be in the back room. There'd be me, Brian Jones, Keith Richards, a couple of other guys in the next little room. And I remember going in and talking to him and playing him some of the *Sgt. Pepper* album. He said, Oh I get it, you don't want to be cute any more! That summed it up. That was sort of what it was. The cute period had ended. It started to be art, that was what happened. Dylan brought poetry into lyrics so you found John doing his Dylan impression on "You've Got To Hide Your Love Away". We were highly influenced by him...

He'd heard "I Wanna Hold Your Hand" 'cos it was Number 1 in the States, but he thought in the middle eight where it said, 'I can't hide, I can't hide, I can't hide', it said, 'I get high, I get high, I get high'. He said, 'Love that one, man, I get high.' He was well into it. And so I had to say, 'No, actually, it's I can't hide...'"

*(Interview: Paul Du Noyer)*

# Muff Winwood

*"Stevie Winwood, he came to see us in Manchester. Last time we were in Manchester...that was 1966. Or was it Birmingham? His brother – he's got a brother named Muff – Muff took us all out to see a haunted house, outside of Manchester, or Birmingham, one of those two...or was it Newcastle? Something like that. We went out to see a haunted house, where a man and his dog was supposed to have burned up in the 13th century. Boy, that place was spooky..."*

(Bob Dylan to Jann Wenner in *Rolling Stone*, November 29, 1969)

*Just where was that haunted house? And was it really spooky? Muff Winwood, once bass player in the Spencer Davis Group and now Head of A&R at CBS Records in the UK, remembers that night very well indeed.*

"Dylan was playing in Birmingham with The Band on the famous face-slapping tour. I was in the Spencer Davis Group then, and he'd heard our records and when he came to Birmingham he wanted to meet us. We were going to the concert anyway, so we just met him backstage before the show...

Anyway, while we were backstage, he was telling us how he was really into ghosts and he loved Britain because of the history and everything and he thought there'd be some wonderful ghosts around. And we knew of a very old massive house in Worcestershire, near Kidderminster I think, that apart from the gatehouse, which was occupied by a caretaker, was left abandoned. It had been burnt and left with all the rafters blackened. And we

73

told him how the guy that had lived in the house had died with his dog, and how if you went there you could see him walking around with the dog. And he was absolutely fascinated with this story and he said, Listen, after the gig you've got to take me to this place! There was just me and my brother Steve, and I thought, Bloody hell!

But after the gig they'd got the limos ready and so we just jumped into these limos – there we were in four bloody stretch Princess limos all driving out to Worcestershire at 12 o'clock at night! Well, we got to the place, so I jumped out and flagged all the limos down and I said, Look, there's somebody living in the gatehouse, so we'd better turn all the lights off and just go in very quietly. So one by one, all these limos turned their lights off and drove carefully through the gates and up the long, long drive to where the house was. We got all the limos up there without anybody in the gatehouse knowing.

And out poured Dylan and the band and girlfriends and hangers on and we started wandering around. The house looked absolutely magnificent – it was a clear night with a great moon and everything, and Dylan was just absolutely knocked sideways by it, just enraptured by it. And of course the classic happened...

We said, Let's all be very quiet, let's see what we can hear. And in the mists there were these old statues in the garden that had got ivy growing all over them and they looked really eerie... and somewhere a dog barked!

Now this is likely to happen in the countryside in Worcestershire at gone midnight, but Dylan is convinced that he's heard the ghost of the dog! He was like a kid! He amazed me because I looked up to this great man, but he'd just keep running up to you and grabbing you by the arm, saying, This is unbelievable! This is fantastic! Really child-like enjoyment of the whole thing. It was great fun..."

*(Interview: John Bauldie)*

# Photographing Dylan

## Elliott Landy interviewed by Paul Williams

*Photographer Elliott Landy's work has appeared on famous LP sleeves* – The Band, *Van Morrison's* Moondance *and Bob Dylan's* Nashville Skyline. *Elliott took some remarkably candid shots of Bob Dylan and his family in Woodstock in 1968, '69 and '70, many of which were published in his book,* Woodstock Vision. *This interview was conducted in New York City on November 3, 1987.*

*How did you get to meet Bob Dylan?*

One day Al Aronowitz called me up in New York. He needed a photograph for the cover of the *Saturday Evening Post* and he said, "Can you come up and do it?" And I said, "Sure." So that's when I met Dylan, when I went up to shoot the cover of the Saturday Evening Post. I went up there and I see him in his environment and he's got a guitar and he says, "Come on – we'll take the picture over here." And he's sitting there playing the guitar and I'm thinking, Boy, probably millions of people would give their right eye to do this and... big deal! It just doesn't mean anything to me...

*You weren't a Dylan fan, particularly?*

I wasn't focused on Dylan, is, I think, better than saying I wasn't a fan. But just the idea that he was sitting and playing the guitar five feet from me – I just saw the paradoxical irony of that.

*How was he to shoot the first time?*

Difficult. He was camera shy – that's why he doesn't want pictures taken of him. He doesn't like being photographed. It's very hard to photograph him. Very hard. When someone doesn't like to be photographed there's some kind of basic insecurity there that comes out. Everyone has it, but it comes out in different people in different ways. Bob, well he was secure in every other realm of his life – in his music: he knew what his music was about, what his poetry was about, he knew who he was as a being, but he was insecure about being photographed. I mean, that's my interpretation of it. Maybe he wasn't; maybe it was nothing personal; maybe he knew that once he was photographed, 13 million people would think about him and maybe he wanted to avoid that...

*But he posed with the guitar...*

He was very co-operative. He wanted it done and we went from the guitar to sitting on his equipment truck and then he invited me back to do some more the following week. So I went back there and I don't remember if I stopped over at his house that first weekend, but I went up there for three or four weekends to do different photographs and he just invited me to stay over. He didn't have to do that. And we had long conversations about different things and got along quite well actually. I got to take pictures of him and his kids, which he had never allowed before.

*What did you talk about?*

Mostly politics, I guess. I was into politics and I'm the kind of person that... I believe everyone's telling me the truth. And he was saying stuff that I believe is true now, and when I told someone about it they said, Oh, he was putting you on – one of the guys in The Band, Richard Manuel; 'cos Bob said things... I don't even know if I should say it publicly, but he said some stuff that didn't make sense to me. Of course, one thinks that Bob Dylan is a very political guy, but quite clearly he wasn't. He's a psychic guy. And he told me that he's a master of language – that he knows how to handle the language very well and that what he was writing about was just what was in the air, which means you pick it up psychically, intuitively. So he was just getting this stuff psychically, and he knew how to handle the language to make it into music and poetry. I mean, that I believe totally. But as we were talking about politics, he says that he's not really very political. And I said, "Well how can you not be political and write those songs?" And he says, "I'm real good with language and that's just what's in the air – that's what people are talking about."

*But he was curious about what you thought about politics?*

Oh yeah. He doesn't talk very much. He wants to hear – he needs people to find out what's happening, you know? He knows he knows what's going on in his own mind – he's very happy, very strong about his own opinions and it's hard to change his mind – once he's made it up, that's it. But he likes to listen, which is a very good quality in a human being. The down side of it is you can't really get a straight answer out of him sometimes. I really like him a lot. I had a nice, friendly, close connection with him. I assume that's why he invited me. 'Course, I didn't realise at the time who Bob Dylan was, so to speak – that it was impossible to get to this man, and everyone wanted to.

*So you were up there for maybe three or four weekends in the Spring of '68?*

Well the times are confusing. I'm not sure when it was exactly, but I decided to live in Woodstock at that point because I knew Dylan and I knew The Band and I had friends up there and it was also a work situation. And so I thought I may as well move up there. And it was nice. Woodstock is a very womb-like place. It's very special there; the feeling is wonderful. It's filled with personal spiritual growth opportunity there – the spirits are very thick, I guess you'd say – and people who go to Woodstock are transformed, people who live there. And Dylan was going through a transformation, I feel, learning love and learning to feel love and to express it and experience it in the family way. That's what *Nashville Skyline* was about – very introspective, very country-like, very haven-like music.

*There are a couple of photographs from '68 of him sitting at the piano. Did he play for you?*

Yes. God knows what – I don't remember. I was just having lunch there and that was what was happening – he wasn't posing, he was actually doing it. He never really got into playing music for me or anything.

*When did you see him again, after those photo sessions?*

Well, I used to see him occasionally here and there, bump into him in the Grand Union or something like that, and then he called me to come over and do a picture for the back of his new album, which he was gonna call *Nashville Skyline,* and he had the cover already picked out – which turned out to be the back, the picture of the *Nashville Skyline.* And he showed me that picture and said that he just wanted a picture of himself to go on the back of the album. So that was the next time we photographed.

*Nashville Skyline* we did for about four days or so, maybe two different shoots. We didn't know what to do; we had no concepts – we just winged it. And it worked! It started out terribly painfully and hard – very difficult. We couldn't get anything good. He was very uncomfortable being photographed and I was uncomfortable photographing him – it worked both ways. And we just stayed with it and we got a moment that was very special. A lot of the other pictures are very boring and silly looking, and that picture was magic.

*Tell the story of that picture.*

Well, one afternoon I guess I went over to his place, and we were taking pictures in the front and the back and walking around. And we were walking through the woods outside the back of his house and it had just been raining and there was water on the ground and... oh, the jacket he has on in *Nashville Skyline* is the same one he had on for *Blonde On Blonde* and *John Wesley Harding,* and the hat he's taking off is also from *John Wesley Harding* – they're just little icons he likes to carry with him, I assume. So we're walking through the woods – we've got boots on, I guess, it's wet out there – and he carries this hat; in the house he said to me, "I'm gonna take this hat, I wore it on this other album." And he just gets this inspiration: he says, "Take a picture from down there." And I start to bend down, I look down, and it's muddy there. I mean, he didn't really want me to go in the mud – it was the angle he was thinking about. So I looked down and saw this mud there – but I didn't even think about it, I just kept doing it. Of course, as he's saying it I'm taking pictures all along as I'm going down there and getting the right angle, and he's saying to me, "You think I should wear this hat?" And I'm saying, "I dunno," as I'm taking the photograph. You know, he's smiling because he's a goof – "Should I wear this silly hat?" So it's kind of a joke that we had going between us about the hat.

*When I've seen the picture, what it always looked like is like he's saying hello.*

Well, what it is is his positive energy: he was in a real good mood, it was sunny out, he was just taken over by instinct – we weren't thinking about anything, we were just having fun. And what comes through is that it's a very loving photograph – he looks very loving – so the love is what shines through. The interesting thing is that when we were looking at the photographs he spotted it. He said, "That's the one!" as soon as he saw it. I had a technique for picking out pictures where you hold up a white sheet the same size as you want to use the photograph, so we were looking at it like that. The minute he saw it he said, "That's the one!" And I agreed. It was the one.

You know, the first time I knew I was gonna be famous was when I knew that my name was gonna be next to Dylan's on *Music From Big Pink*, because they told me he was gonna do the cover and my pictures were gonna be on the inside, so I knew that everyone would look to see his name in the credits, and right next to it would be my name. But then because our names were so similar, anagrams of one another, lots of people thought I didn't really exist at all – that I was him, under another name!

*You did some shooting with him again with his kids, 'cos there's photos in* Woodstock Vision *that say they're from 1970.*

Yeah. That was just a personal thing. Al Aronowitz was up – this was when Dylan moved houses. He changed houses from the old Byrdcliffe house he used to live in, which was his first house in Woodstock as far as I know. He got a much bigger, brighter house. And he wanted me to photograph his drawings – he had a whole sketchbook of drawings that he needed photographs of, so he called me to come over. Actually I think it was a couple of different occasions; I was there once to photograph his drawings and I was there once with Al Aronowitz. We were setting up a trampoline. I don't know how come I was there. It was just to hang out.

*But you always had a camera.*

Yeah, sure. I think he told me to get the camera, actually. I would never walk into his house with a camera without being asked to take photographs. I never pushed taking photographs with him. I never called him up and said, Bob, let's take some pictures – it was always at his request. I was shy about taking photographs of people. I didn't want to intrude on their privacy. I still am. So he really wanted those pictures taken. He was using the camera too. When we photographed I had a few different cameras, so I gave him one, and he was taking pictures of a horse's tail, and he took a couple of pictures of me and a couple of the kids I think. He was interested in using the camera – I don't think he did much with it. He's a great painter, though. Really. Really. Great sculptor also.

*Sculptor?*

I've seen some mindblowing stuff that he's done. I remember one cream pitcher – or maybe it was a cup – no, a cream pitcher, where the handle goes into the middle of the pitcher. Instead of the handle going off on one side of the cup to the other, the handle went from the bottom of the cup into the middle of the cup instead of to the edge of the cup – right down into where the liquid went also. Real brilliant turn around. And there was something that he did with stained glass – a clown – that when you passed it... it wasn't great because it wasn't framed properly, it wasn't displayed right, but when you looked at it, it was quite incredible what he did, in the sense of colour and form. And his paintings I remember seeing a lot. When he lived in New York he showed me his paintings. I've seen the original *Big Pink* painting and it's incredible. It doesn't look so good on the album cover – I was never impressed with it – but the original is stunning. Stunning. Whatever it is, it's stunning. As is the *Self Portrait* original too. His painting is really good and his drawings were like Van Gogh. I mean, it's the same hand. He started painting when he was in Byrdcliffe. His neighbour was a painter and taught him how to use the tools of painting. That's what you do in Woodstock.

*So you were still in Woodstock when you did the trampoline picture...*

Next time I saw him after that period was in New York City. He moved down to MacDougal Street, I got a loft in SoHo. And he came over a couple of times – I think he wanted prints of the pictures I had taken. He came over in disguise. I remember looking out the window, because I had no doorbell, and seeing him with this ski cap on pulled all the way down over his forehead so no-one could tell who it was. He was with his son then I think. Then he and Sara came over to me and Lesley, and we had a nice time, and they invited us to come over to the house. Then he asked me to photograph his daughter's birthday party, and I went over there, and we were getting very friendly. We took his daughter to stay at our loft one time because they were going out of town, and it got strange there and she got unhappy – she didn't like it there, so she called and they sent someone to pick her up. What happened was that we had some people over and his name came up in a conversation, and I didn't realise the extreme paranoia – I was aware of it a little bit because I'd become aware of the number of people wanting him, physically, not sexually, but physically wanting him – to touch him, talk to him. I remember Sara saying to me one time, You wouldn't believe what people do... – just beside herself. And so I wasn't aware that Maria would be sensitive to people talking about him. So she was disturbed by that, and neither I nor Lesley realised it. Anyway, after that period he went to California and I went to Europe and we lost touch completely. That was the end of it.

I wrote to him a few times from Europe, to try to get permission to use certain photographs I had taken of him, which I always could have used, but when I was taking the pictures of him with the kids, we talked about... not me – he said, "We'll have to do a book with these." And I said, "Sure." We talked about it, but it was his suggestion, 'cos I would not have suggested doing a book with his family pictures. And he said, "Yeah, we'll have to do some words and pictures – maybe in about five years or so, when they're not recognisable any more," 'cos he was afraid of kidnapping and generally didn't want to focus attention on his family, because it was bad enough that attention was focused on him, being a very private person. So I would write to him from Europe, but never got any answer. But I had always maintained the right of artistic integrity, just personally, to use my pictures in a personal photographic work – that was my understanding, a verbal understanding. I never talked about it directly with Bob, but Bob was telling me to use the pictures, and Bob was more free with the photographs than anybody else was.

*But it seems that Dylan was unhappy with the picture of his daughter naked that you included in your book* Woodstock Vision.

I don't know which picture it was, but he called me when he saw the book and was very upset – he said Sara was very upset – and at the same time he said that he was looking for some pictures of him and his kids to use on *Biograph*. Now out of deference to his wishes I had waited all that time to use them, even though I wasn't legally or morally bound to do that, because when we took the photographs we talked about using them. We took them to be used. But I respected his problems in life, respected who he was, and felt that he deserved to be consulted on stuff like that. And I was always offered a lot of money for things like that and I'd gone through some hard times myself where I could have used it. I never did it. But always I had made it clear to Albert Grossman's office that I retained artistic right to use them. They were part of my art. But the pictures I took of Bob, the additional ones, I was a friend...

*So this phone call, the only time you heard from him, he initiated?*

Yeah. He said that they were very upset about it, and I assume it's the one of his daughter naked because he was just gonna use pictures of himself and his kids for the first time also. So as he was ready to go, my life also brought me to the point where I was ready to go with the pictures – it was 12 or 13 or 15 years already, it was history. So it was time. The kids were grown up. There was no damage it was gonna do. So I'd upheld what I thought was my responsibility – more than upheld it.

*But if you do another edition of the book?*

I probably wouldn't put that picture in there, even though I think it's one of my best photographs of him. His daughter looks like an angel and his kids look like two cherubs. And it's a very angelic, very spiritual, very beautiful photograph, regardless of who he was – Bob Dylan or not Bob Dylan. It's a picture of a man with two angelic beings. It's one of my favourite photographs. But if it's gonna be that painful for one human being... I could see not publishing it.

*So that was it?*

Yeah. He'd just called to yell at me. He was very pissed off. He didn't even tell me which photograph they were objecting to – I'm just assuming that was the photograph. It couldn't have been all of them. They're very favourable pictures of him – they don't make him look weird, they make him look quite nice, loving and fatherly. I've not had any contact with him since.

# Johnny Cash

"Bob and I had a correspondence before we met. We wrote each other a lot of letters. There's no big secrets in them, but it's a period of Bob's life right after he first started. He had his first album out when I discovered him. I was working joints in downtown Las Vegas, the Nugget and places like that, and I was staying up all night playing Bob Dylan after I got through. So I wrote him a letter care of John Hammond at Columbia and I got a letter right back from Bob in New York. I fired one right back and then he wrote me one from California, then one from Hibbing, one from Woodstock. It was just rambling thoughts, you know – what he was feeling about things, and looking forward to meeting me. I was the same. I was writing him letters on airplanes and mailing them in those vomit bags. I never have shown those letters to anybody, even June. Bob Dylan's a very private person and he would really be embarrassed if I did. I have probably a dozen or more locked in my vault. I would never let those letters out of my vault. Nobody but me even knows where they are in the vault – and nobody's got the combination. I will eventually destroy them."

*(Interview: Bill Flanagan)*

# The Mysterious Norman Raeben

## by Bert Cartwright

Norman Raeben was one of the most influential people in Bob Dylan's life. It was Norman Raeben, Dylan said, who, in the mid '70s, renewed his ability to compose songs. Dylan also suggested that Norman's teaching and influence so altered his outlook upon life that Sara, his wife, could no longer understand him, and this was a contributory factor in the breakdown of the Dylans' marriage. It's strange that, given the importance of Norman Raeben's influence on Bob Dylan, he isn't even mentioned in either of the big biographies published in the 1980s.

Dylan first began to talk about Raeben in the round of interviews he did in 1978 to promote his movie, *Renaldo & Clara*, though for a while he wouldn't specifically identify him. "There ain't nobody like him," Dylan told Pete Oppel, of the *Dallas Morning News*. "I'd rather not say his name. He's really special, and I don't want to create any heat for him."[46] He was, Dylan told *Playboy*'s Ron Rosenbaum, "just an old man. His name wouldn't mean anything to you."[47]

Dylan's interest in Norman began sometime in 1974, when several friends of Sara came to visit:

> They were talking about truth and love and beauty and all these words I had heard for years, and they had 'em all defined. I couldn't believe it... I asked them, 'Where do you come up with all those definitions?' and they told me about this teacher.[48]

Sufficiently impressed, Dylan looked up the teacher the next time he was in New York. It was the Spring of 1974 when Dylan popped his head around Norman's door:

> He says, 'You wanna paint?' So I said, 'Well, I was thinking about it, you know.' He said, 'Well, I don't know if you even deserve to be here. Let me see what you can do.' So he put this vase in front of me

and he says, 'You see this vase?' And he put it there for 30 seconds or so and then he took it away and he said, 'Draw it'. Well, I mean, I started drawing it and I couldn't remember shit about this vase – I'd looked at it but I didn't see it. And he took a look at what I drew and he said, 'OK, you can be up here.' And he told me 13 paints to get... Well, I hadn't gone up there to paint, I'd just gone up there to see what was going on. I wound up staying there for maybe two months. This guy was amazing...

When Dylan looked back upon what happened during those two months, he came to believe that he was so transformed as to become a stranger to his wife:

It changed me. I went home after that and my wife never did understand me ever since that day. That's when our marriage started breaking up. She never knew what I was talking about, what I was thinking about. And I couldn't possibly explain it.[49]

Dylan talked about Norman at length to Pete Oppel, describing in more-than-casual words how Norman taught in his eleventh-floor studio in Carnegie Hall:

Five days a week I used to go up there, and I'd just think about it the other two days of the week. I used to be up there from eight o'clock to four. That's all I did for two months...

In this class there would be people like old ladies – rich old ladies from Florida – standing next to an off-duty policeman, standing next to a bus driver, a lawyer. Just all kinds. Some art student who had been kicked out of every art university. Young girls who worshipped him. A couple of serious guys who went up there to clean up for him afterwards – just clean up the place. A lot of different kinds of people you'd never think would be into art or painting. And it wasn't art or painting, it was something else...

He talked all the time, from eight-thirty to four, and he talked in seven languages. He would tell me about myself when I was doing something, drawing something. I couldn't paint. I thought I could. I couldn't draw. I don't even remember 90 per cent of the stuff he drove into me...[50]

It seems, then, that Norman was more interested in metaphysics than in technique. His teaching dealt with ultimate realities which could be expressed in a variety of modes. It is not certain that Norman made Dylan a better painter, but he clearly changed Dylan:

I had met magicians, but this guy is more powerful than any magician I've ever met. He looked into you and told you what you were. And he didn't play games about it. If you were interested in coming out of that, you could stay there and force yourself to come out of it. You yourself did all the work. He was just some kind of guide, or something like that...[51]

It was some time later when I was finally able to identify Dylan's mysterious man called Norman as Norman Raeben, born in Russia in 1901, who visited the USA with his family when he was three years old and emigrated for permanent residence when he was about 14. Norman's father was the noted Yiddish writer, Sholem Aleichem (1859-1916), a man best known today for having created the character Tvye, whose fictional life-story was adapted for the musical, *Fiddler On The Roof*. The most remarkable change brought about by the months Dylan spent in Norman Raeben's studio was upon the way Dylan composed lyrics.

Dylan told *Rolling Stone*'s Jonathan Cott that following his motorcycle accident on July 29, 1966, he found himself no longer able to compose as freely as before:

Since that point, I more or less had amnesia. Now you can take that statement as literally or as metaphysically as you need to, but that's what happened to me. It took me a long time to get to do consciously what I used to do unconsciously.[52]

Dylan reiterated the point to Matt Damsker:

It's like I had amnesia all of a sudden...I couldn't learn what I had been able to do naturally – like *Highway 61 Revisited*. I mean, you can't sit down and write that consciously because it has to do with the break-up of time...[53]

In the interview with Jonathan Cott, Dylan described his albums *John Wesley Harding* and *Nashville Skyline* as attempts:

...to grasp something that would lead me on to where I thought I should be, and it didn't go nowhere – it just went down, down, down... I was convinced I wasn't going to do anything else.[54]

It was in this mood of near-despair of ever composing as he once had, that Dylan had the "good fortune" to meet Norman, "who taught me how to see":

He put my mind and my hand and my eye together, in a way that allowed me to do consciously what I unconsciously felt.

The time with Norman helped Dylan's psyche be redirected sufficiently for him to write some new songs, the songs that were included on what is still his most celebrated LP, *Blood On The Tracks*:

> Everybody agrees that that was pretty different, and what's different about it is that there's a code in the lyrics, and there's also no sense of time...

Dylan made further efforts to explain the concept of "no time" in the new songs to Matt Damsker:

> *Blood On The Tracks* did consciously what I used to do unconsciously. I didn't perform it well. I didn't have the power to perform it well. But I did write the songs... the ones that have the break-up of time, where there is no time, trying to make the focus as strong as a magnifying glass under the sun. To do that consciously is a trick, and I did it on *Blood On The Tracks* for the first time. I knew how to do it because of the technique I learned – I actually had a teacher for it...[55]

In the *Biograph* booklet, Cameron Crowe's comment on *Blood On The Tracks* seems to be the product of an uncredited observation by Dylan himself:

> Reportedly inspired by the breakup of his marriage, the album derived more of its style from Dylan's interest in painting. The songs cut deep, and their sense of perspective and reality was always changing.[56]

"Always changing" is the product of the LP's sense of no-time. Speaking to Mary Travers on April 26, 1975, Dylan commented upon the concept of time, the point he tried to make being not only that "the past, the present and the future all exists", but that "it's all the same" – something learned from Norman, Dylan told Jonathan Cott, who used to teach that:

> You've got yesterday, today and tomorrow all in the same room, and there's very little that you can't imagine happening.[57]

Dylan's assertion to Matt Damsker that he didn't perform the songs on *Blood On The Tracks* particularly well may be surprising but, he went on, "they can be changed...". In fact, Dylan has continually reworked the songs, changing the lyrics again and again in such songs as "Simple Twist Of Fate" and "Tangled Up In Blue". Dylan ties up ideas of time and change to the idea of song-as-painting with specific reference to "Tangled Up In Blue" on the jacket notes to *Biograph*, where he says of the song:

> I was just trying to make it like a painting where you can see the different parts but then you also see the whole of it. With that particular song, that's what I was trying to do... with the concept of time, and the way the characters change from the first person to the third person, and you're never quite sure if the third person is talking or the first person is talking. But as you look at the whole thing, it really doesn't matter.[58]

The dissolving of persons and of time in the *Blood On The Tracks* songs was a remarkable achievement; Dylan was to try to apply the same technique when he made his film *Renaldo & Clara*. In tracing the influence of Norman Raeben's thinking, Dylan called Jonathan Cott's attention to *Renaldo & Clara*:

> ...in which I also used that quality of no-time. And I believe that that concept of creation is more real and true than that which does have time...
>
> The movie creates and holds the time. That's what it should do – it should hold that time, breathe in that time and stop time in doing that. It's like if you look at a painting by Cezanne, you get lost in that painting for that period of time. And you breathe – yet time is going by and you wouldn't know it. You're spellbound.[59]

Small wonder, then, that Dylan was most annoyed by those who criticised the film's length, and perhaps it is not inappropriate to mention a more recent statement of annoyance – at those who tried to pin down one of his no-time, no-person songs from *Blood On The Tracks*:

> "You're A Big Girl Now", well, I read that this was supposed to be about my wife. I wish somebody would ask me first before they go ahead and print stuff like that...[60]

Dylan once unconsciously created songs with the no-time quality of painting. Many times he spoke of parallels between song and painting – one recalls, for example, Dylan's introduction of "Love Minus Zero/No Limit" in concerts in 1965 as "a painting in maroon and silver" or "a painting in purple", but only after studying with Norman Raeben was he to recapture his apparently lost ability to write such songs, now with the notable difference of conscious composition. And if *Blood On The Tracks* was to be the first attempt to translate what Dylan had learned from Norman into song, it was *Street-Legal* which Dylan would come to regard as the culmination of the insights into the nature of time as no-time. As he told Matt Damsker:

> Never until I got to *Blood On The Tracks* did I finally get a hold of what I needed to get a hold of, and once I got hold of it, *Blood On The Tracks* wasn't it either, and neither was *Desire*. *Street-Legal* comes the closest to where my music is going for the rest of time. It has to do with an illusion of time. I mean, what the songs are necessarily about is the illusion of time. It was an old man who knew about that, and I picked up what I could...[61]

# Patti Smith

## by Miles

*Patti Smith, poet and rock singer extraordinaire, was in bed in the Chelsea Hotel when Miles called round to ask her about her encounters with Bob Dylan back in 1975. The interview was conducted on March 18, 1977 but never published.*

In 1975, at the Other End, when we played there, right after me and my band got signed, Bob came. I knew he was there – nobody had to tell me. I felt something. The neat thing about him is that his energy is a real thing. I don't expect anything out of anybody when I meet them, all I expect is that... if I've really admired them... that they exude a certain kind of energy that's really inspiring. And he had a lot of it. He's really an amazing storehouse – he's so full of grace, speed and urgency, it's a real thing.

I'm never ashamed to say what makes me happy, and that was something. It was really great. And then he came back to see me and it was different because there was the same kind of sensation that I used to have in high school, like when you meet a guy in the hallway... it was just like that – teenage. It was like we had an energy collision. I felt like we were both... blue T-birds, you know, having a head-on collision. Or like a pit dog dance, or a cock fight, circling around. Then I got real nervous and I went to another room – and he came after me and said something. And I moved to another room and he came and hugged me and people took pictures. It was really great, just like when you're the wallflower all your life... I always wanted to dance with boys and nobody ever asked me to dance, I had to wait for ladies' choice and I'd always pick the most beautiful boy, the most popular guy – I was so pathetic. But Bob understands that, 'cos he wrote the song "Wallflower" and he knew me, y'know, and he was checking up on me. Not as long as I'd been checking up on him!

At that time he was going through... he had been in hiding for so long, or... it wasn't the '60s any more. And Dylan had been King of the '60s, the Absolute King – he had Elvis Presley's crown of thorns, he was the next in line, the successor for the championship of rock'n'roll. To me, Dylan always represented rock'n'roll – I never thought of him as a folk singer or poet or nothing. I just thought he was the sexiest person since Elvis Presley – sex in the brain, y'know? Sex at its most ultimate is being totally illuminated, and he was that, he was the King. And he still has it. I don't think his true power has been unleashed. I haven't stopped believing in him.

Well, he wanted to come out, and in the club he kinda saw in me someone who was potentially as strong as him, who has a lot of energy – the kind that makes you totally uncomfortable with the world – and he recognised that. On stage I was into improvising, linguistically, and I was especially inspired that night because he was there. But of course I learned that from him, from "Bob Dylan's 144th Dream Of Captain Ahab", and yet it was almost like it was a new thing to him. I said, "You have to remember where that came from!" He started getting really turned on by the idea of the band – my guys following me or pushing me and not faltering or wondering about what musical changes to go into because I've just spread the song out like a hand. He saw somebody doing something that he didn't think was possible, and he said, "I wish I would have stayed with just one group – if I'd had the same group all this time how well we would have known the ins and outs of each other."

He started hanging out more. He liked the fact that he could be in a club and people didn't maul him to death, because there were a lot of things happening at that time. And we were all hanging out there, and it was really great 'cos we'd all get drunk and stuff and be falling around. People just started turning up in the Village. It happened very fast. Jack Elliott was around – everybody was around. Then one night, Bob started going up on stage, jamming with these people. I saw him start getting attracted to certain people – Rob Stoner, Bobby Neuwirth – it was great to see him and Bob back together because he really brings out the worst in Dylan, which is what we usually love the best. And he was working out this Rolling Thunder thing – he was thinking about improvisation, about extending himself language-wise. In the talks that we had there was something that he admired about me that was difficult to comprehend then, but that's what we were talking about. That's what we were talking about on the stairway – there are pictures – when he started getting Rolling Thunder together.

Everybody was asked to go on Rolling Thunder except me. And then he told me to come to this party. Actually I thought he was inviting me for a drink – he asked me to come to some bar at Gerde's Folk City, where he first started in New York. So I went, and there's a million people there – well known people, and I thought he was asking me for a drink, he couldn't have asked all these people – is this a coincidence? But it was a party for a birthday and they were also going to announce Rolling Thunder.

And how he announced it was real weird. First, him and Joan Baez got up and sang "One Too Many Mornings", which was one of my favourite Dylan songs...now you see, I'd seen him a lot in between all this time, but it's like personal, y'know, not relevant – only to my memories... Anyway, different people got up: Bobby Neuwirth, Jack Elliott got up, Jim McGuinn got up and sang his horse song; Bette Midler got up and sang this song – she didn't do such a hot job. She may have been nervous – at first I thought she was just obnoxious and not so hot, but she did this weird thing – she came over and threw this glass of beer in my face! Just walked up! I never met her before. It was like a John Wayne movie! She had bloomers on – or pyjamas, I don't know. I was real shocked. And then Dylan stood right up and he made me go up there. But I had no band, no song prepared, but I understood that why I had to go up there was to save face. Since I couldn't hit her I had to do something to maintain my dignity, so I got up there and Eric Andersen was there, and I said, "Just play a droning E chord behind me." So I just made up this thing. I looked at Bob, and made up this thing about brother and sister. But while I'm doing it I start thinking about Sam Shepard – he was in my consciousness – and so I told this story, really got into it, made this brother and sister be parted by the greed and corruption of the system – I did a good job and lots of people liked it. I was real proud. There was a lot of tension. Phil Ochs was there, and Phil Ochs could always bring out that *Don't Look Back* side of Dylan. Dylan's got that side still – it's all stored up – he's all those people, he's still that guy, he hasn't turned beautiful and gentle, he's real bastard – but that's what I think is great, for his art – maybe not for being a husband! And he was like really a son-of-a-bitch that night. Phil Ochs was crazy. Phil Ochs... I couldn't believe it, but Bob wouldn't talk to Phil Ochs. The two of them... it was like there was a noose in the middle of the room and they were circling around, trying to get each other to hang themselves.

One time he was telling me what my gifts were – he has great humility but he doesn't like flattery – hates for you to tell him how much he meant to you all your life, through your young years – he doesn't want to hear that. What he wants to do is tell you the good things about you, so that you can do your own work; he doesn't want you to be involved with him, he would rather inspire you to do your own work – he's not jealous and possessive about that. So he was trying to teach me just what my worth was, and we did some neat stuff together. They were filming this, at a crazy party up on 8th Street somewhere. He told me to maintain the eye of an eagle, which he told me I had, and then Phil Ochs came up and poured a whole pail of beer on my head, and Bob started fighting with Phil and I said, "What *is* this? Every time I'm around you I get doused with beer!"

The next step was that I had to go to a rehearsal at S.I.R., the last rehearsal. And he's singing these songs and I wanted him to rock it up. I said, "What's with this acoustic guitar?" Then he goes off into a room. But then there's like these hot-shot lawyers and bodyguards and stuff around – it looks like the Mafia – I can see why he was into Joey Gallo – he has himself this whole thing – and they tap me on the shoulder and they go, "Bob wants to see ya!" And so these lawyers take me on into this room and he's standing there, looked great, and his lawyers say, "Bob is having this Rolling Thunder Revue and he wants you to go on it." And he says, "Erm .. yes. I think it would be very good for your career – get you exposure." And I thought it was a riot, him talking to me like that! And I said, "Whaddya mean? Exposure? I'm getting well exposed! You didn't discover me under a rock, you know – people know I'm out there!" And I said, "Look, you got 150 million people going on this tour with you, you don't need to make space for me. I'd just drive you crazy, totally crazy. And the only thing I'd ever want to do with you is to drive you crazy – to push you so far that you would start to cut everybody down verbally, that you'd play the best solo on the electric guitar, push you to see you be the best, not rehashing old folk songs and singing country harmony – I ain't interested in singing country harmony with you, I did that in a bar, where country harmony belongs."

Well, he saw my point. I'd got everything I need from him – he's inspired me for so long. I guessed it was time to turn the beat around. So I said, "I'll give you one tip. Use your fists." He sort of hung his hands when he was singing, when he was standing there without a guitar he didn't know what to do with his hands. I said, "Grab that microphone. You got these fists, you're singing about a boxer, Hurricane Carter, use those fists! Box with them. You're a great mover – what're you standing there like a dead fish for? Move!" He was a great mover in the '60s, Dylan, those great little curtsies he used to do. I said, "You're the father of Cool. Don't be cool by being uptight, be cool by moving with the moment." And he says, "Aw, I can't hit the air with my fists or nothing. People will think I'm copying you!" I said, "Well, I've imitated you for 12 years, you can spare a little imitation." So he just laughed. Seeing him laugh is great, 'cos he has a lot of pain. He's like the Duke Of Windsor – how he gave up his crown for the woman he loved, y'know? He's like that. But he's also got a streak in him that won't give up being a contender, and the streak is what gives him so much life – that streak makes him keep creating, keeps putting him out there.

Anyway the streak took him out on the Rolling Thunder thing. Sam went out on the road with him, I didn't go. Sam did the same thing – kept pushing him to improve, got him to Kerouac's grave, got him to exorcise his demon and to really start celebrating. And Dylan opened up – his lungs, his sunglasses became windows – and then he slammed them shut again. And Sam said, "If you're gonna get involved in all this superficial folky stuff then I'm leaving." So Sam split. I couldn't believe Sam split. Dylan's not used to having people walk out on him. He didn't like it.

Dylan's such a fucking maniac. Y'know, I've not said anything specifically, but I hope I've done something here to remind how intense he is, and how much that intensity has only been successfully revealed through abstract expressionism in rock'n'roll. I look at him and I don't see a guy giving out leaflets, holding a banner. I see a machine gun.

# Joel Bernstein

## Interviewed by John Bauldie

*Joel Bernstein is a photographer, guitar technician and musician. He has worked closely with many artists, especially Neil Young, Joni Mitchell and, most recently, Prince and Tracy Chapman. And Bob Dylan, of course. He was interviewed for "The Telegraph" in London in November, 1989.*

*How did you come to work with Bob Dylan?*

I had been playing guitar on tour with David Crosby and Graham Nash in 1975, and after that tour I ran into Barry Imhoff – it was just after Bob Dylan had played the Houston Astrodome and they'd had a disaster where the guitar technician had miscalibrated his strobo-tuner so the entire set was totally out of tune – way out, apparently. So Barry said, Oh listen, we might have something for you. And sure enough they called and asked me to do the guitars for the second Rolling Thunder tour. And I'd heard about the first one – I had some friends who were on the film crew – and I thought, God, this sounds like the most exciting energy going on here. I was thrilled to be asked to do it.

*So when did you start on the 1976 Rolling Thunder tour?*

The rehearsals were in the Starlight Room of the Bellevue Biltmore Hotel in Clearwater and they went on for some time before the tour. It was somewhat strange. Bob would show up late for rehearsals, he wouldn't talk to the band, he'd just start a song. I never liked Rob Stoner's playing very much but I have to give him credit. He really understood, could follow Bob by looking at his foot, following his heel, listening for the first note and then he'd get a feel for the key,

Backstage at the De Montfort Hall, Leicester, during the UK tour of May 1965.

Above, left to right: As Bobby the Hobo in the BBC Television play 'Madhouse on Castle Street', tele-recorded 30 December 1962, broadcast 12 January 1963 (*BBC Television*); Dylan's first professional engagement, supporting John Lee Hooker at Gerde's Folk City, New York, 11 April 1961; On stage in Stockholm, 29 April 1966; A promotional shot for Fender guitars, taken at Columbia Studios, New York, December 1965—Fender supplied instruments to Bob Dylan and the Hawks for the electric tours of 1965 and '66 (*CBS Records*); With Bob Johnston during the recording sessions for *Self Portrait* at CBS Studios in Nashville, 1969.

Dylan receiving his honorary Doctorate of Music from Princeton University, 9 June 1970. The occasion was later the subject of the song 'Day of the Locusts' on *New Morning*. (Top left) On stage at the Westphalia Hall in Dortmund, West Germany, 27 June 1978. *Horst W. Mueller*. (Top right) Saved! 1980. *Susan Wallach Fino*

(On) stage at Western Springs Stadium in Auckland, New Zealand, 9 March 1978.
(Inset) On stage at the Fox-Warfield Theatre in San Francisco, 22 November 1980.

*Nancy Cleveland*

On stage at Wembley Stadium, London, 7 July 1984.

*Willem Meuleman*

(Top) On stage at Wembley Arena, London, October 1987.
*Susan Wallach Fino*

(Bottom) On stage in Atlanta, Georgia, 25 July 1988.
*Mauro De Marco*

During the filming of *Hearts of Fire*, September 1986.
*Lorimar Telepictures*

and the rest of the band took their cue from him. Bob spoke very little – he wasn't talking to me for a while – and it seemed a very strange way to proceed with rehearsals.

*How long did the rehearsals last – a couple of weeks?*

Weeks and weeks in the Starlight Room. The Bellevue Biltmore was the oldest still inhabited wooden structure in the United States – an old Victorian Hotel from the 1880s – and there were something like 65 salaried tour people, which was amazing, plus various hangers on. And the rehearsals went on for quite some time. The first rehearsals were in the poolhouse, and that proved to be too small, so after a day or two we moved into the ballroom, which of course they had to pay more money for.

Usually rehearsals began around noon and Bob wouldn't show up until two or so and not say anything, just pick up a guitar and play a song. My impressions were that he was either angry about something or that the whole thing was getting old for him. It was just a mood he was in.

*They made a film in the ballroom of the Bellevue Biltmore...*

Yes, the *Midnight Special* TV show. There were two takes of it, which I thought were very good. He'd only let them film it by buying out the rights to the show so that he could have approval on its release or not. Well, his solo sets were great – the band stuff I didn't care for that much. There were too many guitars going on at once – it was cluttered. Throughout the tour there wasn't a great camaraderie happening with the band.

*I must ask you about that outrageous white National guitar that appeared on that tour.*

That guitar was a terrible guitar. That was the first one I'd seen of those. It was in the shape of the USA. Bob called that guitar "Rimbaud". He had us put "Rimbaud" on it – we got a book of Rimbaud and cut out the name and attached it to the guitar. When he wanted that guitar, Bob would ask for "Rimbaud".

He had a beautiful little Gibson guitar, old guitar, and he came to rehearsal one day, played one song and put it down, leaning it against a chair, and left. The chair was outside on the verandah to the ballroom and the sun was out, so as guitar caretaker I brought it inside, re-tuned it, and put it back on its stand. Couple of hours later he came back and said, Joel, could you do me a favour? I said, Sure, Bob. He said, The next time I put a guitar down, could you just leave it where it is? It really confuses me when you start moving things around. That was the first conversation I had with him. My introduction to his own strange kind of logic.

Shortly afterwards he brought in a guitar that I hadn't seen before. It was an old Martin, an O or OO, that he wrote on – he never played it in concert. The strings had obviously not been changed in a long time, certainly over a year – they were completely dead. So naturally I re-strung the guitar. A little while later, Bob came out saying, Joel? What did you do with those old strings? I *liked* that sound! Can you get 'em back? Can you put 'em back on the guitar? I said, Oh gee no, Bob, but I can try to make these as dirty as the old ones. In fact, in his guitar cases you'd find these ancient strings all carefully wrapped up – strings that you would never want to use again. I guess it was a throwback to his old folky days when you couldn't afford to buy new strings.

*You're credited with the video still that was used on the back of the* Hard Rain *sleeve. How did that come about?*

I think it was Howard Alk's suggestion. Of course, when I went on the Rolling Thunder tour I was told that I couldn't by any means take any pictures of Bob, even though they knew I was a photographer. Well, needless to say, after the first three shows it was, Joel, do you have your cameras? Bob wants some pictures taken tonight... Anyway, they wanted to have some shots of Bob from the video at Fort Collins for the LP sleeve and I had come up with this technique of photographing from video using still frame using a Hasselblad, 'cos videos weren't good enough to give a still picture that was free from noise at the time, and Howard and I went through the video looking for various things we could shoot. I'd shot a lot from the front, but the background was very cluttered with all the scaffolding and the paintings, so it wasn't a very pleasing thing to be looking at. The shot from the back just happened to be one that I stopped at. I never thought it would be used. As a matter of fact, that picture doesn't look like a video still, it looks more like a pointillist painting.

*So did you never get the chance to photograph Bob offstage on the 1976 tour?*

No, I don't think so. As I said, it was only towards the end of the tour where he'd even say hi or how'r'y'doin' to me, or act, er, normally. In fact, it was good training. It's stood me in good stead since I've been working with Prince, because he's another very intense person who communicates a lot with looks and who doesn't have time to talk to you but who expects things to be perfect.

*Does Bob have perfectionist expectations?*

Oh not really, not compared to Prince. When I say he wants things done right, he just wants to be free to do his thing without having to worry about whether his guitars or his amps are going to work. I was pleased that I made him very in tune. I certainly think that I tuned Bob better than he had ever been tuned before.

Actually, I've just been reminded of a story of when Mick Ronson was trying to get Bob to use some pedal effects, a wah-wah, distortion and so on. So he took some of his effects and set them up in Bob's line and said, Go on, Bob, just try it! So Bob walks over to the pedals and he said, Those things? Mick says, Yeah, you just step on them. Bob says, Yeah, but, er, will it make me sound like Buddy Guy? Hahahaha! And that was the end of that.

*You mentioned the paintings on the sheets at the back of the stage on* Hard Rain. *Can you recall Bob painting those?*

The paintings were done by Bob and Bob Neuwirth, I think just for that show. I thought Bobby Neuwirth was very full of himself, like, Oh, Bob likes me. Very self-important way beyond his abilities. He'd bash away at the guitar and always break strings.

Sara and the kids came to the Fort Collins show – I seem to recall that even she had a turban on. And I do have a shot of Bob on that day onstage with Jesse underneath the stage – a vertical shot with the two of them, Jesse, aged eight, looking at me.

Was the gig that the Revue did at the Texas Boys Reformatory ever reported? That was the only show in 1976 that Joni Mitchell played on. It was not a scheduled gig and not a publicly attended show. And do you know that the opening act at the show in Tampa was Steve Martin, the comedian? He did a stand-up set. By the end of the '76 tour...actually, the last show was Salt Lake City, and Salt Lake City...this is probably on somebody's tape list...

*Salt Lake City's a very elusive tape...*

Salt Lake City was the only show that I recall that Bob and Joan did "Lily, Rosemary & The Jack Of Hearts" together. The song has something like 18 verses, and Bob wrote the first lines down on the back of his hand, on his cuff, on his sleeve... They did a very good version of it, really good. It was a very spirited show, perhaps because it was the last show. People knew that it wouldn't happen again.

*So what came after the 1976 tour?*

Well, we come then to *The Last Waltz*. I'd been on a Neil Young/Crazy Horse tour which finished in Atlanta the day before *The Last Waltz*, and I'd got a call, a frantic call, from the producers of the show. Apparently, nobody who was working there had worked with Bob and they were afraid that he was going to not have things together and maybe decide not to play at the last minute. So they asked if I could come and set up his gear and take care of everything for the show.

I'd been up all night, took the red-eye into San Francisco and set up a small rehearsal in a room, a banquet room, at the Miyako Hotel for Bob and The Band. Bob came in that afternoon and I was the only one there and what was funny for me was that when he came in it was like he was my long-lost friend. He was like, Oh Joel! How're you doing? You been working with Neil? He said more to me in that one afternoon probably than on the whole Rolling Thunder tour.

Well, they played for hours. Actually, Neil Young came in later on and just sat and watched with me. And it was just a great thing to witness. They tried a number of different songs together. And I had brought my camera equipment but I wasn't allowed to shoot at the rehearsal of course, and I had to move all the gear over to Winterland for the show. So I did that and I then set up my tuning station, 'cos I was also going to be taking care of Neil Young and Joni Mitchell, and in fact I finished up doing all the guitars for everyone except for the initial tuning of The Band and Eric Clapton. Anyway, during Bob's set I was crouched behind one of the Fender amps on stage and you can see me in the film.

I think it was because I had helped out at The Last Waltz and we'd got along together that I was asked to set up rehearsals in 1977 at what became Rundown Studios. He had just rented the place – at the time it was an office building where they'd made *Saturday*

100

*Night Specials* downstairs and there was a computer manufacturer upstairs. And he wanted to change it into a rehearsal space, so we rented a piano, amps and all of that and there was just me and another person working there at the time. I wound up actually living there from about September 1977 until we left for the Japanese tour early the following year. Bob actually had a room too. I turned one of the offices into my bedroom and he had an office that was set up as a bedroom too. So that was when I spent the most time with him, because there were auditions and rehearsals all the time. There were members of the band that he knew that he wanted, like Steven Soles and Rob Stoner, but he was looking for other players – he needed a drummer and he auditioned a number of drummers, maybe 10 or a dozen. It was an interesting experience for me, watching all these different musicians trying to play Bob's songs. I remember Bob had to go out and get the *Writings And Drawings* book, and he would flip through it, stop at a page and say, Oh yeah *this* one! Let's try this one! Remember *this* one? It was really a treat to hear him try different things.

He was much more disciplined than I would have imagined, by contrast to the 1976 tour. Not only was everything taped but he would have the band stay over after rehearsals finished and he would have me play back particular performances of the best versions of each song that day that either I would pick or he would pick, and spend an hour, hour and a half, listening back to things.

*How long were the rehearsal sessions themselves?*

Rehearsals would usually begin about one o'clock. We would get some soup from a good soup place right nearby, a bakery that had fresh rolls, and put it in a crockpot and people would show up and have lunch and then we'd start around one and play until six.

Of course, the band got bigger as time went on, and once it was reasonably together he got them to play certain songs in different ways, in one key and then another key and then half-time, then country, then reggae, then rocked up. It was really an experimental thing. And then listening to those songs he would just pick one, say, Yeah! That's the one! And I would inwardly groan and go, Oh no! Not the *reggae* one! But he had his own ideas about what was the best one to do. And perhaps some of the complaints about those shows being too slick came about as a result of the songs being rehearsed so much compared with other tours. And of course the size of the band, and the stage itself was fairly modern – it was actually a very nice stage to work on – and the outfits, the black and white theme, probably put some people off.

*You took photographs of those 1978 Far East shows...*

I took the photographs on the sleeve of the LP *At Budokan*. It was originally for Japanese release only since his last album in America had been *Hard Rain* and CBS was just not interested in another live Bob Dylan album, so my original negotiations for the pictures was with CBS/Sony, but then CBS bought the rights to it but they changed the cover photograph. They put some contrast on it to change it somewhat so it looks different than it did on the Japanese release.

I have a lot of offstage shots. I just found a whole series of Bob at a shushi restaurant – no, a shobi-shoba restaurant, a whole series of him with a waitress. That's really something. He looks fantastic. The whole tour was taken out by the promoter. It's a funny series. I have a shot of him playing his guitar in the transit lounge of the Hong Kong International Airport. He wasn't so isolated on that tour as he had been on Rolling Thunder.

*So what else do you have stashed away in the Joel Bernstein archives?*

Well, Cameron Crowe gave me a set of his original liner notes for *Biograph* with Bob's corrections and comments in the margins. Those are great. Some of the things Bob wrote about the early days especially are just really incredible. Which reminds me, I'm the person referred to at the beginning of the *Biograph* liner notes about going to a Bob Dylan party. That was me.

I also have a demo of "Every Grain Of Sand" with him and Jennifer Warnes and a dog barking in the background. Oh my God! It just kills the record. Graham Nash was sent a copy of it for some reason, maybe by the publisher thinking he would sing it or something. For some strange reason he had a copy of it and he let me copy his cassette, and it's just fantastic – it's Bob on piano, Jennifer Warnes on back-up vocal and this dog singing in the background. And it's such a great version of the song – definitely one of the best things I've ever heard. It's magical.

*So at the end of the Far East 1978 tour...*

I was laid off, right after we came back, much to my surprise. I don't know why. They were just going to set up the studio for *Street-Legal*... before I forget, I did the shot on the inside of *Street-Legal*, which is Bob and George Benson at a nightclub in Melbourne. They both happened to be in the same restaurant and I shot it in much less light than there is under this table... anyhow, that was the last time I was hired by Bob, 11 years ago.

*Have your paths crossed since?*

I ran into him backstage at one of the *Born In The USA* shows, just said Hi! I saw him, I think the last time, at a rehearsal of his with Tom Petty's band in Los Angeles. I listened to about an hour of that. One thing that was really great was when Bob started playing "Come Together", which the band had never played before. They did an incredible version of it and never did it again. To hear Bob doing a John Lennon song – wow! I was lucky to be there.

# Bob Dylan & Renaldo & Clara

## by Allen Ginsberg

*When Allen Ginsberg, on his way home from Hawaii, called in to see Bob Dylan in California in September 1977, he found him hard at work putting the finishing touches to the editing of* Renaldo & Clara. *Intrigued and delighted by what Dylan was doing, Ginsberg promptly resolved to write a critical appreciation of the film. He asked for Dylan's co-operation, watched the film several times and then conducted a lengthy interview with him, in which the film's aims, objectives and symbolism were discussed. However, at the interview's conclusion Dylan told Ginsberg that he thought he had "revealed too much" and demanded that Allen give him the tape back.*

*Then, between October 27 and November 1, Ginsberg again tackled Dylan about the film. At the same time, Dylan was also interviewed by an otherwise unidentified figure named Pierre Cotrell. I have edited what follows from transcripts of these interviews. The Pierre Cotrell interview, the occasion for which is uncertain, took place in two parts on October 30. Later, in his preliminary editing work, Ginsberg mixed the Cotrell papers with his own and it is not always easy to identify the questioner. When it is certain that Cotrell is the questioner, this has been identified by the bracketed name (Cotrell), otherwise it is to be assumed that the questioner is Allen Ginsberg.*

*In generously giving permission for the interviews to be printed at last, Allen Ginsberg wishes it to be noted that he has had no hand in the preparation of the material for publication. The interviews are prefaced by a draft, unfinished prose introduction to* Renaldo & Clara *by Allen Ginsberg. (John Bauldie)*

# A DRAFT OF AN INTRODUCTION TO *RENALDO & CLARA* by Allen Ginsberg

*"Peace of Mind, All Passion Spent" – Milton*

*"For this Relief, much thanks, for tis Bitter Cold and I am sick at heart" – Shakespeare*

*"Tell all the truth but tell it slant, Success in Circuit lies"*
*– Emily Dickinson"*

Signs above were chalked in Bob Dylan's hand on blackboard basement wall, large room filled with editing tables, indexed film cans on metal shelves, & box with filing system breaking down reels into subjects & themes, personages, recurrent images, a hand sorting system for retrieving linked images notated on filecards in the two year process of viewing and editing, composing, the 4 hour film "Renaldo & Clara", a task which Dylan shared with Howard Alk as he had previously shared composition of the hilarious Chaplinesque speedy film "Eat The Document" all the funny faces & slapstick oneyed comedy of a previous decade summed in youthful essence, & rejected by aging TV Moguls as too far off the wall. Lighthearted punk comedy, innocent playfulness accommodating the viewer, blacksuited Zimmerman slapping his spread fingered hand to his face staggering away from his piano's instant rhapsody. And inviting the camera viewer to sit down & relax at the end film.

"Renaldo & Clara" thus a continuation of film & poem techniques of linked images explored by Alk & Dylan deliberately. We didn't just sit in the basement 2 years, we worked, Dylan explained carefully. The entire occasion hundred-person electronic tour Rolling Thunder from this aspect an occasion magick'd up for film, to create a bank of images (as in Cocteau's Surreal pioneering barebones filmed theater Blood of a Poet, with its battle of snowballs & glistening black angel Dargelos the cock of the class & snowy balcony full of silent applauding furred & tailed aristocracy). The composition also resembles Burroughs method of gathering images for different thematic novels in different manila files till one or another Mr Bradley Mr Martin, Cities of Red Night, Wild Boys, Nova Express etc assemble to critical mass.

The themes isolated early are abstract classic obsessions peculiar to Dylan's domestic thought, a set of neutral Universalities, applicable to anyone's thought, permutated in chains of linked flashing images, in cinema talk, hooked into each other on many levels – indian song to Indian face painted on sound truck rolling thru technicolour rain; a "travelling vagina" that is a crimson rose flower hooked from scene to scene held in ladies hands or sniffed at by truckdriving dreamers – images that reappear in different surprising contexts beginning to end. The Composition is interlacings of hooked themes (rose Indian etc) recurrent characters, varieties of the main identity Renaldo and his different personae ie the hatted whitefaced man who sings on stage, the silent walker or exhausted self stretched on the floor dreaming, etc; and locations or image-places. The themes originally lined up in a gamut of archetypes as follows: Dreams, Money, Love & Men & Women, Marriage, Children & Mother, God, Poetry & Music, Sex, Death, Rolling Thunder Review, Pilgrims & US, Indians, Prophecy & Teachers, Jewishness, Prison, Police, Kidnapping, Sighs, Dogs, Lying & Truth. Some themes disappeared in the long process of elimination of unbeautiful or unlinked or brilliant but unhooked bits of intelligence. This then is the language of the film. Dylan editing and directing has accomplished what Alk sees as a breaking open of the film language, doing to cinema what Dylan has done to song, linking the gifted images in meanings that are conscious and unconscious, linking sound with sight associations, whole areas of blue predominant, then red; following a story of mirrory similitudes shot to shot, many subtle threads woven into fabric culmination or surrounding a song (one of 42 entire or fragmented & quoted throughout the movie) that comments on a recurrent theme.

In some respects the texture is that of a realistic dream, with quick changes and shifts, & obsessive totems repeated in different form, truckstop conversation of life as doing good time or bad time like in prison, later followed by heroine Clara bringing her man an escape rope to climb over prison wall & run away scared thru the city, coat held masking his mouth.

A constant event is the shift of roles: The actor Bob Dylan playing the Character Renaldo who dreams up the whole show while playing out a part searching for his identity; the actor Ronnie Hawkins playing a rough-egoed would-be seducer named Bob Dylan; Joan Baez playing Death the Woman in white: these roles will be discussed later from the horses mouth: Dylan was eager to make imaginative interpretation of the basic nature and function of his dozens of characters, their comprehensible roles in relation to Truth. All relate to truth, ie as the Chorus in the Truckstop Diner says, Truth is not lying to yourself (& thus doing good time, something real).

In sum Dylan has found a Masque, or panorama of personified principles – The Father played by myself, the Son played by cherubic pedal steel musician Dave Mansfield, angel wing'd & haloed half naked in a Bordello in Diamond Hell, Clara the Eternal Feminine Freedom fighter played by citizen Sara Dylan; and the film character Mrs Dylan (fighting with her tour boyfriend who hasn't copulated with her in 3 years) played by brilliant Ronee Blakely.

These are the basic elements of composition of this work of art, classic modern in its mode, reflecting early XX century painting practice – simultaneity, attention to 2 dimensional optic field, recurrence of totemic pictures, collage or cut up ie jump cuts shot to shot thematically related without linear plot logic, except the b plot be the slow examination of faked & illusory identities as Renaldo the hero tries to experience them one after another, all the possibilities of his vast dream in which he tries to catch up to the present, and leave behind a past that never was, a past that is all vanished, like a dream, a figment of memory, an arbitrary conception, a prison of thought habit.


BOB DYLAN INTERVIEWED BY ALLEN GINSBERG (and Pierre Cotrell)

*What attracts you, as a poet, to movies? What do you look for?*

To shift my consciousness somewhere – hopefully to a place that applies to my own personal experience. I want to be entertained. If I see a movie that really moves me around I'm totally astounded, I'm wiped out. If film was around when Da Vinci was operating, he'd have made film... I consider myself like Da Vinci. Film is an art medium nowadays, but art didn't become Art till the 19th century; it existed 3,000 years before it was "Art". Before the 19th century people painted what they were paid to paint. They weren't painting anything individual. Look at Bosch – there's no struggle. There's no struggle in any of Dali's painting. Life is a struggle. If you want to do business and create work, then you struggle; if your struggle shows, then you make it. It's all about hard work, ploughsharing. Even Van

Gogh used what was there – he never painted what he would've liked to paint. He painted what was there to paint.

We try to make something better out of what is real. If we want to be successful as an artist, we make it better, and give meaning to something meaningless.

*What's your idea of "Better" – your direction of "Better"?*

You can make something lasting. You wanna stop time, that's what you wanna do. You want to live forever, right Allen? Huh? In order to live forever you have to stop time. In order to stop time you have to exist in the moment, so strong as to stop time and prove your point. So that you have stopped time. And if you succeed in doing that, everyone who comes into contact with what you've done – whatever it might be, whether you've carved a statue or painted a painting – will catch some of that; they'll recognise that you have stopped time – they won't realise it, but that's what they'll recognise, that you have stopped time. That's a heroic feat! We have literally stopped time in this movie. Um hum. Regardless of what it's about – Renaldo and Clara, a guy selling a horse, a guy singing on a stage or fighting with a man, whatever it is – we have stopped time in this movie. We've grasped that time. And we are the only ones. I've never seen a film except one other that has stopped time.

*What film is that?*

"Children Of Paradise".

*Yes, I thought that, sure!*

And this movie stops time in a way that no American movie ever has and I don't think will. What we've done is hold on to something which seemed to be escapable, and we captured it and made it real. You notice how everybody watches that movie and says, "Jesus, it just seems like yesterday; it seems like this happened just the other day."

*Do you want to be immortal? And why?*

I'd like my work to survive, yeah. Do you remember what Henry Miller wrote on that? "An artist innoculates the world with his disillusionment." It's not good enough to be an observer all the time. You have to know that you've stopped time. You think about nothing. You're totally absorbed in what you're doing.

Any singer can do that. Some fake it. When it resolves itself, it's never resolved – you have to resolve it. To resolve is nothing more than letting go. Do you think Rembrandt ever finished a painting? I mention him 'cos he seems to be a perfectionist – I'm saying he let go. He has got many layers underneath. Rembrandt made mistakes too.

Look how long it took to build the Pyramid... When you wrote *Kaddish*, you had to let go.

*(Howard Alk)* The poet has classically spoken in the First Person.

I use I and me and you. It's personal. All the great movies stop time for you. You're standing in awe in front of the painting the painter has achieved. Through the art lies immortality. That makes him high, gives him everything he needs, just knowing he can do that. How many people can say that, that they've lived their life? The artist couldn't care less about who sees it. You see it, you know it, yeah. It falls off on the observer. I don't think you're a conscious artist, Allen. I don't think you know what you're doing. Anybody can be an unconscious artist – I am a conscious artist.

*What do you mean I'm not a conscious artist? Are you a conscious artist?*

Yes. Because I had a teacher that was a conscious artist and he drilled it into me to be a conscious artist, so I became a conscious artist.

*A painting teacher?*

Yeah.

*And what does a conscious artist practise?*

Actuality. You can't improve on Actuality. Let's say that this is what God gives you – he gives you a flower. *(Dylan offers a flower).* Let's see you improve it. *(Ginsberg, confused, tries flower arrangement. Dylan says he means "improve" it by photographing it or singing it.)*

*What is* Renaldo & Clara?

109

Reality and Actuality transcending itself to the final degree of being more than the Actuality. Renaldo is the actuality, and what the film is is transcending Renaldo to a higher Actuality and Clarity. Renaldo is everybody. Don't you identify with Renaldo? Renaldo is you, struggling within yourself, with the knowledge that you're locked within the chains of your own being. Actuality is what is.

*What is Clarity?*

Anything that's clear.

*What's Renaldo's basic situation?*

He maintains, lying on his back. He's Everyman in the movie, and he survives. He is a man contemplating the future. His situation is he's pulling away from his past, but how does he get away from a past that doesn't exist? One of his characteristics is that he goes everywhere. At the opening of the movie he's in a mask you can see through – it's translucent. At the end, he's seen putting on face paint. Renaldo is a figure of Duality. The Mexican man who traded the horse was the other side of Renaldo's Duality. The man who puts the white paint on his face obviously becomes the Chorus of the movie. He has no name... The man on the floor at the end is the Dreamer. That's neither Renaldo nor the Chorus nor the man on the stage – the stage is part of the Dream. A man who's walking around seeming to be alive has dreamt nothing. But the man on the floor, who's obviously dreaming, no one asks him anything – but the whole movie was his dream.

*What's the significance of the scene where the College Kid, when asked, says he had no dream last night?*

This whole movie is the dream that the College Kid did not have. This whole movie has gone down and they haven't dreamt any of it. The movie that you never dreamt, that you wish you'da dreamt.

*(Howard Alk)* The movie you haven't dreamt yet.

*Does Renaldo have a soul or is he a succession of disparate illusorily connected images, like ordinary mind?*

At the beginning he's locked in, he's wearing a mask you can see through, he's not dreaming. Most likely he will become what he's dreaming about. Renaldo's dream almost killed him.

*It's at the end of the movie, when he's putting make-up on – "What you can dream about can happen".*

Exactly! You got it! Renaldo has faith in himself and his ability to dream, but the dream is sometimes so powerful it has the ability to wipe him out. Renaldo has no ordinary mind – he might not even have a soul. He may in actuality be Time itself, in his wildest moments.

*What about Clara?*

Clara is the symbol of Freedom in this movie. She's what attracts Renaldo at the present. Renaldo lives in a tomb, his only way out is to dream. Renaldo first appears in a mask, then he's told in the cafe, "That's the way it is." Lenny Bruce said, "There isn't anything that should be, or what's supposed to be, there's only what is." All there is, is what is – we're not used to that in modern times. If you want to summarise the film, this is the way it is: "There are heroes in the seaweed".

*What holds Renaldo in this inescapable tomb?*

Compulsion. You know at the end of the movie he's about to or has broken out of that tomb... you feel that even though he may be under strenuous times, he might transcend them. Renaldo has no regard for man, woman or circumstance; it is only his dream which keeps him going.

*What compels Renaldo to Clara?*

Her abandonment. He's attracted to her freedom. I don't know if I should say superficial freedom. The entire world is in chains according to Clara – bondage to themselves, slaves to their ego. She helps Lafkesio get out of prison. Everyone is Lafkesio to her. Renaldo to her is the only person in the entire world who isn't Lafkesio – that's what attracts her to him.

*Why is Renaldo dreaming up all this confusion and disturbance and activity and music and masquerade?*

He's trying to break out of himself – not only that, he's trying to break out of himself by means of reason. He's not a logical minded person, but he does believe in the reason of his own soul and the ability of his own soul to reason, and that's why the masquerade is continuing... He's also trying to recognise his soul.

*What if there is no soul?*

*(Dylan smiles)* Then the whole journey has been in vain.

*What if it is in vain! What if that's the liberation?*

Then the journey that we're all on has been invalid... He's actually in the process of conquering his own soul.

*That could be interpreted variously.*

What can't be?

*Why end the movie with the black singer singing "The Morning Of Your Life"?*

Because it's in fact the morning of Renaldo's life. He has ceased to be Renaldo. From that moment on he will become what he wishes to become. No more will he answer to Renaldo. Renaldo wants to be free from his unforgettable past – in other words, he wants to forget his unforgettable past and something earthshaking must have happened to him.

*Is that earthshaking event in the film?*

It's represented by the whole series of events in the film.

*Who does Renaldo think he is?*

He thinks he's anybody but Renaldo. What time does he have to think? He dreams. He doesn't think. Thinking would make him a logical man. He's not thinking, he's only acting and dreaming.

*What comments does he make on himself in the film?*

He doesn't make any obvious comments. I haven't heard him make any. You don't see him as a man of obvious personality or characteristics, you see him as a man either driving or being driven – either you're hounding or being hounded. Do you remember him getting off the bus and running with the woman screaming in his head? He witnessed a lot.

*Did you make this movie as a representation of yourself, psychologically?*

Yes. Is this too intellectual?

*No. Mature men talk about their experiences. So these characters are all dream projections of Renaldo – all aspects of the mandala of his own ego?*

Yes. Exactly.

*Why does Renaldo think about himself so much?*

We don't even know if he's thinking. Renaldo doesn't even think at all. That's his aura. Renaldo might not even think. It may be that's what they're projecting on him.

*Everybody wants a piece of Renaldo, seeking his heart. Does he encourage it? Does he recognise and work with his creation consciously, with the characters, this appeal to their hearts and vice versa? Is everyone trying to be his companion so he won't be alone or so they won't be alone?*

He anticipates it. They really don't care too much about Renaldo – whether he's alone or not – they're only thinking about themselves, which is exactly why Renaldo's heart is breaking. See, the thing is Renaldo comes closer to himself towards the end of the film – and there he is with Bob Dylan's wife, sitting on the train near the end of the film.

*What does that mean – that he's just going out with girls or something?*

Well, you've got to take into account the look on people's faces.

*What about the Woman in White?*

It's the ghost of Death – Death's ghost. Renaldo rids himself of death when she leaves, and he goes on, alive, with his greasepaint. He's becoming the hero of his own dream. The Woman in White, the Joan Baez persona, exists only in Renaldo's imagination in this movie. The Woman in White first appears at the end of the first half, after Renaldo restates his point that "It ain't me, it ain't me babe." That's when the god forces bring in the big cannon – The Supreme Ego, White Death – and try to make him fixate on that.

*When does she have the rose?*

Immediately. She's carrying her cunt in her hand.

*Her first words...*

You hear resonating in her head. "Once you start lying to yourself, you become an enemy to yourself." The issue at hand is lying to oneself – not just false advertising. Her first line is "Is Renaldo there?" She's come for Renaldo – he's in her mind's eye. She's travelling towards him. She won't leave when he's making it with Clara. She always seems to go, but she never goes. She must leave three or four times, but she's always back. You see her standing there.

*How can he get rid of her?*

Through transfiguration. She finally leaves. If you see the film, notice all that finally happens to her. For instance, this woman is the ghost of Clara's former self. She is this same woman who was traded for a horse. Now during that time Joan Baez and Dylan – the man in white paint and the past that's non-existable – sing a song, "Never Let Me Go"; and when they're looking at the newspaper, their minds are headed to the same point. Renaldo's closer then to being face to face with what he knows and loves and being able to discard it. Our ego becomes so strong sometimes that we believe it and begin to listen to it. The ego does cling to the past.

*Does every word in the movie count?*

Sometimes yes, sometimes no. There are many other elements in the movie, beyond the character of Renaldo. It's the movie of Renaldo, but there's so much action passing through his experience – like the figure of The Masked Tortilla, a guy of Heroic proportions capable of Heroic deeds: like in the nightclub where he's taking the stand for this man who can't articulate. It's an example of something he can do – a Heroic nature, a modern day Robin Hood. On the other hand, he's capable of great compassion and great self-pity – haunted by it but brave enough to break out of it. He's also a dreamer. The man who's singing in whiteface, he's a dreamer, and that is his sidekick, confidant, and he's also a dreamer. But his dream is not as big or tangled as Renaldo's. Basically, his dream is black and white, good and bad – opposites like that. Nothing is happening in the movie except one scene – the singer at the end, who's been singing since the beginning of the movie, is in another room, another time, another era, but in the same breath. It's his songs which are special, it isn't him.

*Isn't Renaldo like everyone, alone, flat on his back? Is this the Show of Alone? Is it a moment of Rest?*

It's the moment where Renaldo's beginning to understand himself and what's been happening to him. By the time he understands himself, the Woman in White has vanished completely – she no longer exists in his dream or in his reality. Now for further information you have to check the movie.

*The Woman in White represents Death exonerated? The Duality of... a stagnation?*

Renaldo's obsessed with his own freedom. Clara represents that obsession. Clara's coming out of church with a rope, to get somebody out of prison. To her, the whole world is in chains; everyone is in bondage. She herself is an example of supposedly attainable freedom, but is she really free? She's the one that's gonna stay in that room. Clara's becoming an enemy to herself. You notice she's gonna stay in that room. Renaldo, applying white greasepaint, is going to get out. Clara has no dream.

*How can he leave her if she symbolises freedom?*

She's a part of his past. In order for him to survive he must leave her behind.

*Is Clara free of her ego?*

Clara's free, but she can change – she says. We know she can change because we've seen her in different ideas of herself. Renaldo, you only see him dreaming. The man onstage clarifies Renaldo to himself. Maurice, the French Canadian, is a parallel real life figure of an everyday man who's biding his time. He gives Renaldo a shoulder to cry on. Clara is summed up by the words of the Poet as she's coming out of the church – the sorrows of the world are reflected in her eye: "With your eyes of no money/with your eyes of false China/with your eyes of Czechoslovakia/attacked by robots". Everyone in the movie happens to be a poet: Blue was talking about poets; the poet Father is Clara's father; Christ himself – the idea of Christ – might be Clara's brother; Clara might be Christ's sister. How many girls are mistaken for their mother? It's a common occurrence.

*(Cotrell) How do you relate to Jesus?*

He's in the film, especially in reference to the myth of the complete man which exists inside of Renaldo's head. Renaldo's attempting to become a Complete man, to step aside of himself.

*(Cotrell) Is Renaldo the brother of Christ?*

No, he's no relation to Christ, he only dreams of Christ. Christ is a mythological figure on which the movie hangs. There are many figures in this movie, but they go by so fast.

*(Cotrell) There's the Father . .*

The Father, the Idea of the Father, the Voice of the Father, the Necessity of the Father. The Girlfriend's talking with Dylan – says her Father won't let her go off with him; her brother is played by David Mansfield, her son, the angelic boy, a musician, a parody of Christ, the Innocent Lamb. He might be Clara's brother.

*(Cotrell) Parents and children never agree; does this Father agree with his son?*

There's no conflict. The Father cares very deeply for the Son, obviously. He wants to enlighten him into new experience, in the Bordello – the Diamond Hell.

*(Cotrell) Diamond Hell?*

It's not a Bordello. They are part of the past which didn't exist. We're all involved in our past, which didn't exist. My past doesn't exist any more than anyone else's. Why should I be different? Why should I have a past when nobody else has? The girls sitting in that room are a reflection of Nothing and Nobody. They're locked into Diamond Hell and are not giving pleasure to no-one.

116

*(Cotrell) What's the relation of the Father to Renaldo?*

He's taught Renaldo what he needs to do to be a poet, but indirectly. Renaldo, of course, breaks away from the Father – he has no patience with the Father, although he respects him. The Father is actually a figure of indecision. The key line of the movie is "What comes is gone for ever every time."

*(Cotrell) There are lots of ideas of death presented through the movie. Mexican Death – "We may not make it through the night", Kaddish, Kerouac's grave, the discussion about graves visited...*

The idea of death in the movie is really the idea of life, like in a photographic negative.

*Did the characters in the film pre-exist its making, or did Renaldo and Clara emerge during shooting or editing?*

No, no, they were there before the movie even began, otherwise there wouldn't have been a movie. They were there from the beginning.

*Why did Renaldo never really face the camera?*

You mean why are you seeing only certain sides of Renaldo? That's all he allows you to see. That's natural. He looks right at you through the mirror in the final scene. You see more dimension and depth in Renaldo than you do in most films you see. I think this film might be too simple in its complexity.

*(Howard Alk)* It's that you're pursuing, not that he's hiding. He becomes more accessible to you physically. He's masked at first, but the whiteface becomes more and more worn away as the film goes on.

Renaldo's caught in a period of alienation from himself – caught up in the mess of not being able to compete with his other self, the man he is working to become in order to survive the hellhole he's found himself in. The man in whiteface is what Renaldo cannot become at the moment. At the Indian party that isn't Renaldo, that is the man in whiteface. He represents the compelling figure of authority which Renaldo is trying to become. Renaldo is trying to transcend himself, through the past and the present. He's trying to make it into the future, but he can't do that unless he leaves the unimaginable past behind.

*The Indians...*

That's all part of Renaldo's dream – all part of his past experience. The Indian child, who's actually a medicine man, represents the Chief of Practical Purpose, the Chief of practically everything practical, the Chief of Practical Matters.

*Tell me about some of the other figures in the movie.*

The one pure figure in the movie is The Girlfriend. One, she explains that she needs her father's approval to go off with Dylan; two, she offers refuge to Renaldo; three, she tells the musician that there are no gigs left. As the film makes obvious, no one pays any attention to her; no one's going to let her stand in the way. She has all these basic principles of life – she's the one figure of real Truth in the movie. She changes, in the movie, from Innocence to Beauty. She's talking to Renaldo – "Stand and bear yourself like the Cross and I'll receive you". She's actually the one person in the movie thinking more of Renaldo than of herself. She's never got a rose. Her cunt's never displayed.

*You've been talking about the rose . .*

In the symbol of the rose we see the vagina travelling around. You see it a lot. You could trace it every time it comes up. Go to the movie and pick up all the signs where the rose goes. First on the table in front of the truckdriver, who's almost contemplating it; then Clara in one of her former selves – a manifestation of her as desperation – picks up the rose and then travels with it. It was nobody's rose. Clara picked it up and went off alone to the train station, where she sees and lures Renaldo for the first time. We can also refer to the rose as "the dark opening". Scarlet constantly represents the vagina, the rose, the sweetness of it – always at the elusive Renaldo's right hand, that close. The man in the white face, the reasonable Renaldo, can always reach out to grab it.

*Hurricane has a role...*

He represents the Certainty of common sense. He's common sense being ostracised. There's something special about him – he's obviously a philosopher, a philosopher in chains, isn't he? We have this song "Hurricane" and we have this man. It comes back to the idea of getting out of prison. Clara will *do* what Renaldo will only dream about – get a man out of jail. Renaldo may be thinking about it, singing about it, but Clara *does* it, directly, in present time.

## The Old Woman?

She's a gypsy, some kind of healer, an Influence – the Guilt Influence, the Influence of Institution, Marriage, Money, the concept of Money – it doesn't sneak through her fingers – she's a false prophet. She doesn't obviously heal the Father, but she makes the pretence of being a healer. She's very materialistic. She's got the rose wrapped up in her head, as does Scarlet. The movie deals with the transfiguration of the rose, if you can catch that going by.

## What quality do you see in David Blue?

You know in the old Greek plays, the Chorus? David seems to know what's going on, but he's only existing in Renaldo's dream. He's the narrator who links the movie to generational history. I think, though I could be wrong, he's a figment of Renaldo's imagination that attempts to reconcile the past that never was. David Blue has no past. He represents neither past nor future. There'd be no David Blue if Renaldo didn't exist. There's the dream element. The movie is Renaldo's dream. The chorus is the reality of this movie. Take the chorus out of the movie and you'd have no movie.

In the diner, the man who says if you lie to yourself you do bad time, this man lives on experience alone. That's what teaches him. He's a man who learns from experience.

## The Reporter?

He doesn't play any role. He can't get out of the present at all; he can't get to the past or the future. He's locked in the present. He's one of the few people in the movie that survives in the present. The Girlfriend is the only other one.

## Bob Dylan?

You don't know much about Bob Dylan, only one aspect of his personality, for obvious, almost comical reasons. His name is mentioned, he's part of the Rolling Thunder Revue – there's a disc jockey who told you: "Dylan, Baez, Neuwirth, Elliott". Bob Dylan is being used here as a famous name, so we don't have to hire Marlon Brando! But in this case we have the proof. Now he's very obviously a cowboy in a straw hat – someone else is playing Bob Dylan, with a slightly persuasive personality. His aim is to get what he deserves. He makes his intentions very clear. He's not trying to hide anything. You can hear the obvious sincerity in his voice – and also a desperate need to communicate.

*A belly dancer was belly dancing in the room Bob Dylan wanted to get into, and Ronson wouldn't let him pass. Why? Did he want to get into that room to watch, or to belly dance?*

Maybe he was going to make a connection with one of those ladies, or meet someone there at 10 o'clock. Bob Dylan exists in Renaldo's dream. Lafkesio, he's the one that doesn't. He trades his horse, unknowingly, for a woman who's at that moment existing inside a song that the singer in whiteface is singing. The man onstage happens to be Ramon, who's assaulted with a razor by Mrs Bob Dylan, who's been having an affair with another man. One man is accosting a woman who's having an affair, and her husband hasn't slept with her for three years, but he still knows who she's sleeping with. "Then I see the bloody face of Ramon." We don't even know who does Ramon in – Mrs Bob Dylan or Mr Bob Dylan. I suspect it was Mrs, but I'm speaking for the film buff here. In the context of the movie it doesn't matter. After all, if he hasn't slept with her in three years, the heck with him!

*So who's Ramon?*

Ramon actually is the memory of the dead lover, the memory of a bygone lover. Rightly or wrongly, he accuses her of taking on lovers.

*"The bloody face of Ramon"?*

The image of the dead lover. Ramon's on the stage quite a time. You see him in the mirror. He's the Hanged Man – someone who's suspended.

*Why does she turn on him all of a sudden, when he says "I know who you've been fucking"?*

Why? Because he doesn't really give a shit. Mrs Dylan's song in the movie is need, need, need – that's all she does. She sings a song called "New Sun Rising". She needs a new sun rising every morning and a new moon every night. She just needs a lot of that stuff.

*The character played by Helena Kallianiotes?*

Helena represents something – a true figure of mystery or purity? You never know. She really is the unattainable of the world, on the material plane – both attainable and unattainable. She never has a rose, never needs one. She's not gonna take no for an answer. She works in negatives. She doesn't want to be denied. She wants never to get where she's going. She's the lost companion, the companion you never see again.

*There are various other minor characters...*

Ungatz appears four times. He appears in the motorcycle shot on the street. He seemingly doesn't know what's going on. He's a man who can be trusted with anything and it'll be safe. You won't be able to get a word out of him and any word you do get out of him you won't be able to comprehend anyway. So he will give you the time of day and that's all – as Renaldo does. He's a minor character. This is a textbook guide for when you're watching the film!

*What about Rodeo?*

He's an important character. He appears three times. He's perplexed. He exists in a vacuum. He has a preconceived idea of himself – a young man of tomorrow.

*Who's Jack Elliott?*

Longheno de Castro. He's with Renaldo at one time – with that man we can assume is Renaldo – driving a van. He used to be married. He had some kind of scene, he had his moment of blisshood somewhere down the line, and now what he's doing is hard to say – he's kinda locked up in time and space. It's hard to tell what kind of effect it's had on him, but he's looking for answers – looking for the answer that he's already had. He's a continual searcher, a rambler, a bit of a demagogue. He appears at the short scene at the end of the drive, with the woman behind the counter. He says, "I just got married". He's the man who announces to Lafkesio that he's traded his horse for a woman. He can't understand that, obviously – can't understand a man who trades a horse for a woman. The woman's a replica of Longheno de Castro's woman in marriage.

*Who's Bob Dylan?*

Nobody's Bob Dylan. Bobby Dylan's long gone. He's looking into the film editing viewer, asking "Who's this man? Who's that?"

*Bob Dylan had been long gone before you started the movie?*

Yes. Let's say that in real life Bob Dylan fixes his name on the public. He can retrieve that name at will. Anything else the public makes of it is its business.

*(Cotrell) Who are you in the movie?*

Me? Sitting here? I'm not in the movie. I was in the movie when you saw the movie – obviously I play Renaldo. I was Renaldo in the movie. Sometimes I just appeared on the set and happened to be Renaldo. You're concerned with Bob Dylan.

*(Cotrell) But everybody will be concerned.*

I'm not concerned about everybody. Neither is Bob Dylan. Bobby Dylan made a movie. When you go to a movie, do you ask what does that person do in real life?

*(Cotrell) Why did you need to make the movie?*

I don't know. If someone does something, you can't ask him why he did it. I like to go to the beach too. I can fix a flat. I think it's amazing somebody can go out and make a film that's never been made before. I've never made one before... not a big one.

*(Cotrell) In* Renaldo & Clara *the relationship between Dream and Myth is so clouded that we confuse them.*

That's very true! I couldn't say it better. The disc jockey said: "If somebody told you Bob Dylan was coming to town, you probably wouldn't believe it." You notice that? "If somebody told you the truth, you probably wouldn't believe it." But the film is no puzzle, it's A-B-C-D, but the composition's like a game – the red flower, the hat, the red and blue themes. The interest is not in the literal plot but in the associational texture – colours, images, sounds.

*Pound's* Cantos *are constructed in this way – image to image.*

Every great work of art is when you think about it. Shakespeare. The point to get is that the film is connected by an untouchable connective link. I'm as good as anybody to tell you about it for starters. There are some things happening in this film which are literal. There are words for what this movie does, and then again there are no words. I was interested in reading Rona Barrett in the paper: "This movie will do for movies what his music has done to influence American music".

*(Howard Alk)* The grammar of movies is broken open. Now you can make your own grammar.

Individual filmmakers are hard to find these days. What filmmaker watches what other filmmakers make? Howard and I were on to this idea 12 years ago, so it's not like something which just happened yesterday – not just something we did in the basement the last two years.

*(Howard Alk)* There are moments of classical musical comedy – some people are going to be crying, some laughing, some will shut up when the movie's shown.

A crowded theatre's going to be dangerous. There's a moment during "Just Like A Woman" that's as close to Mr and Mrs Bob Dylan as the movie gets. The meaning of the film is the shedding of the skin, just like a snake. If a snake doesn't shed his skin, he's through – he decays. To survive, he must. The film doesn't have anything to do with decay; there's nothing decaying in this film. Basically, this film was made because the makers of it wanted to see it as a film, as an experience. I'll tell you what we artists do: we try to create what we must create, because it isn't there. When have you seen *Renaldo & Clara* before? If it had been done before, we wouldn't have had to do it.

*You chose to do it as improvisation...*

How else? Life itself is improvised. We don't live life as a scripted thing. Two boxers go into the ring and they improvise. You go make love with someone and you improvise. Go to sports car races, total improvisation. It's obvious everyone was acting in that movie for dear life. Nobody was thinking of time. People were told this, this, this – the rest of it is up to you, what you say in this scene is your business, but at the same time beyond that, the only directions you have are: you're going to die in a year, or see your mother for the first time in 20 years. So far as instructions to actors go, less is more. And I made it clear to the cameraman, Paul, that it wasn't a documentary, and I told him not to shoot it like that.

*Would you call it a visionary documentary?*

No. "Documentary" pretends towards objective reality, this pretends to Truth.

*So how would you sum it all up?*

Renaldo's intense dream and his conflict with the present – that's all the movie's about. I'd like to make more movies after this. The next movie Renaldo might be working in a factory, who knows? The next one will be more socially identifiable with. The next one will be different. It will be about Corruption, about Pride, about Vanity, and about Obsession. I'm giving away a lot here. I don't want to give it away.

# Helena Springs

## Interviewed by Chris Cooper

*Helena Springs was a backing singer in Dylan's band from 1978 to 1980. She also co-wrote several songs with Bob Dylan, two of which were later recorded by Eric Clapton for his LP,* Backless.

*Tell me how you came to work with Bob Dylan in 1978.*

Bob was actually my first major gig. A good friend called me one afternoon and said, "I'm auditioning for this guy Bob Dylan". I didn't know who Bob Dylan was. Anyway, she said, "I gotta audition for this guy and I need another girl. Can you audition with me?" So we went as a threesome, auditioned, and I was the only one that got the gig! So I got out of High School right on to Bob's tour.

*When you auditioned, did Dylan have the rest of the group or was he just beginning to get things together?*

He had a lot of the guys already; he had Billy Cross, David Mansfield, Steven Soles, but he hadn't really sussed the girls yet.

*It was the first time he'd actually used a girl chorus for concerts. Did he have any idea what he wanted?*

He said he wanted girls that didn't sound like back-up singers, who had their own individual sound and just didn't blend.

*There are tapes of rehearsals for the 1978 tour and on one of them there's a version of* Coming From The Heart, *which I know you co-wrote with Dylan. Can you remember when you sat down and did those things?*

We started writing together in Brisbane, Australia. We were together in Brisbane one evening and he was just playing on the guitar and we were goofing around, laughing, and he said, "I'll write something with you, we'll write something together" and I said "OK". He said, "You start singing some stuff and I'll start playing." So he started strumming his guitar, and I started to sing and just making up these lyrics, and then he'd make up stuff and that's how we got "I'll Be There In The Morning" (sic) and "Walk Out In The Rain". Then we got "Coming From The Heart", "Red Haired Girl" and a bunch of other stuff – "Pain And Love" – it just kind of kept flowing. "Love You Too Much" came later on, "Stepchild", "Stop Now" we wrote together, "Wandering Kind" which was actually covered by Paul Butterfield in 1982, "Tell Me The Truth One Time", "Responsibility".

*There's a demo tape of you playing those on piano...*

We were trying to get other people to do the songs so we had to put them down. Bob, who knows mostly male artists, gave them mainly to guys – like with "Walk Out In The Rain" and "If I Don't Be There In The Morning" (sic), those were given to Eric Clapton while we were on tour in Europe. We played them to him on guitar in Holland, then we got back to do Blackbushe and he had them demoed. And he had done a great job on them and he asked us if he could do them.

*Did you record many of the gigs?*

Oh they recorded pretty much every gig and if anyone was not doing the right parts or not working right you know, you'd have to hear it that night so you'd be on it for the next show.

*Did Bob choose all the songs or did anyone else make suggestions?*

No, no, they were all his decisions. Sometimes he'd write a song and we'd just get the song at a soundcheck. Like "Is Your Love In Vain?", we got that just like that, you know.

*You did Saturday Night Live, the first time he played any totally religious songs. Can you remember much about when he became a born-again Christian?*

Yes I do. I don't know if I should say or ... hmmm ... it was a chain reaction of things. I can't really go into too much depth, because that would upset me. I think it had to do with personal things. He was having some problems once and he called me and he asked me questions that no-one could possibly help with. And I just said, "Don't you ever pray?" And he said, *"Pray?"* Like that, you know. And I said, "Don't you ever do that?" I said, "When I have trouble, I pray." He asked me more questions about it, he started enquiring, he's a very inquisitive person which is one good thing about him – he's always searching for truth, truth in anything he can find. It was like he was exploring Christianity. He didn't give up being a Jewish person, but he learned how to pray, and when he'd learned all he could learn, he went on to something else.

*Those San Francisco concerts in 1979 were extraordinary.*

Yeah, they were, those 14 days at the Fox-Warfield. I remember a lot of people were ... hmmm ... people from the Vineyard in Los Angeles – it's kinda like a cult, Jesus-type people. I remember a lot of them pressuring him about a lot of things. They were not allowing him to live. I remember one time he said to me, "God, it's awfully tight. It's so tight, you know?" He found a lot of hypocrisy in those Jesus people that he had gotten involved with. He mentioned that to me. I said, "You're going to find hypocrisy in any religion." We had a lot of talks about it.

# Saved! Bob Dylan's Conversion To Christianity

## by Clinton Heylin

> Jesus put his hand on me. It was a physical thing. I felt it. I felt it all over me. I felt my whole body tremble. The glory of the Lord knocked me down and picked me up.[62]

> There was a presence in the room that couldn't have been anybody but Jesus... I truly had a born-again experience, if you want to call it that.[63]

Bob Dylan's born-again experience seems to have occurred sometime during his late 1978 tour of the USA. He'd spent most of 1977 editing *Renaldo & Clara*, itself liberally sprinkled with Christian imagery, and having to come to terms with what proved to be a painful and rancorous divorce from Sara. These were not happy days for Bob Dylan – the songs on *Street-Legal* bear this out – but, just at a time when he needed something to pull him through, he found Jesus – or rather, Jesus found him:

> Jesus tapped me on the shoulder, said, Bob, why are you resisting me? I said, I'm not resisting you! He said, You gonna follow me? I said, Well, I've never thought about that before...[64]

Dylan's subsequent conversion to Christianity was certainly influenced, perhaps even brought about by his then-girlfriend, the black actress Mary Alice Artes, who attended a meeting in Tarzana, California of a religious group called the Vineyard Fellowship. Ken Gulliksen, pastor of the Fellowship, explained:

> At the end of the meeting she came up to me and said that she wanted to rededicate her life to the Lord... then she revealed that she was Bob Dylan's girlfriend and asked if a couple of the pastors would come there and then and talk to Bob. And so Larry Myers and Paul Emond went over to Bob's house and ministered to him.

He responded by saying yes, he did in fact want Christ in his life. And he prayed that day and received the Lord.[65]

Dylan seems to have rapidly come under the wing of the Vineyard Fellowship. He was baptised at the home of Bill Dwyer, another Fellowship pastor, and enrolled at the School of Discipleship where he studied the Bible five days a week for three and a half months. He certainly regarded it as a whole-hearted embracing of a new faith, later telling Karen Hughes:

> Christianity is making Christ the Lord and Master of your life, the King of your life... the resurrected Christ, not some dead man who had a bunch of good ideas and was nailed to a tree, who died with those ideas but a resurrected Christ who is Lord of your life. We're talking about that type of Christianity.[66]

Mary Alice Artes, who had brought Christ to Dylan, was to be thanked in two songs – "Precious Angel" and "Covenant Woman", and indeed the Bible study quickly influenced Dylan's songwriting, at least 10 new songs being written in the first four months of 1979. According to Ken Gulliksen, Dylan had someone to consult about the theological soundness of these new compositions:

> He shared his music with Larry Myers, one of the pastors who had originally ministered to him. I freed Larry to go with Bob as much as possible... he and Bob became very close and trusted each other. Larry was often the backboard for Bob to share the lyrics.[67]

Dylan recorded his new songs in 11 days in May, 1979. *Slow Train Coming*, the first Christian LP, was released three months later. The songs were steeped in the Bible and also showed the influence of a book called *The Late Great Planet Earth* by Hal Lindsey. Lindsey's thesis concerns the imminence of Armageddon, the war to end all wars, in the Middle East, initiated by Russia and her new ally Iran, and the timely return of Christ to prevent the annihilation of all mankind. Dylan not only incorporated Lindsey's Biblical interpretations in his songs but, in a three-part, six-month tour of the USA which began in San Francisco in November 1979 and ended in Dayton in May 1980, Dylan was often to be heard fervently preaching a similar doctrine to enthusiastic, bewildered or downright hostile audiences. There's no doubt that he was encouraged in his evangelism by his pastors from the Vineyard Fellowship, but Dylan's enthusiasm seems to have surpassed even their expectations, as Ken Gulliksen explained:

Dylan is potentially able to reach more people with the Gospel than anybody in our generation because of his history... we strongly encouraged him that he had a platform that no-one else had and that in that position he should continue. We told him to be open to God's leading... We did not anticipate that his ministry would be so radical, probably the most far-reaching ministry of any of the rock generation people.[68]

Here, then, are a few examples of the extraordinary Bob Dylan sermons from those shows:

### Tempe, Arizona November 26, 1979

*(Audience booing and heckling)* Hmm. Pretty rude bunch tonight, huh? You all know how to be real rude. You know about the spirit of the Anti-Christ? Does anyone here know about that? The spirit of the Anti-Christ is loose right now. Let me give you an example. Somebody stopped by my house and gave me this tape-cassette. There's many of these false deceivers running around these days. There is only one gospel. The Bible says, Let anyone who preach anything other than that gospel, let him be accursed. Anyway, a young fellow stopped by my house one day and wanted to so-called "turn me on to" a certain guru. I don't wanna mention his name right now, but he has a place out there in LA. And he stopped by and gave me this tape-cassette, to show me... *(Audience cry of 'Rock'n'roll!!')...* If you want rock'n'roll, you go down and rock'n'roll. You can go and see Kiss and you can rock'n'roll all the way down to the pit!

Anyway... you want to hear about this guru? So. Anyway, this guru, he made a film of himself. He had one of these big conventions – he has himself a convention about once a month. Like, they go off to a big city. So I took a look at this tape and sure enough he was having himself a big convention – he must have had about 5,000 people there, or 10,000 people there. And what he was doing on stage was, he was sitting there with a load of flowers and things. He sure did look pretty though, sitting up there, kinda like on a throne, y'know? Listening to him talk on the tape, he said What life's about is life's to have fun, and I'm gonna show you how to have fun! And he had a big fire extinguisher and he would spray it out on the people, and they all laughed and had a good time. They took their clothes off. They were overjoyed to be sprayed by this man. And a little while after that, he's talking about his philosophy. And he said that he was God – he did say that. He said that God's inside him and he is God. And they could think of him as God.

I want to tell you this because they say there's many of those people walking around. They may not come out and say they're

God, but they're just waiting for the opportunity. There is only one God. Let me hear you say who that is. Their God makes promises he doesn't keep. There's only two kinds of people like the preacher says – only two kinds of people. Colour don't separate them, neither does their clothes.... *(Audience: "Rock'n'roll!")*... You still wanna rock'n'roll? I'll tell you what the two kinds of people are. Don't matter how much money you got, there's only two kinds of people: there's saved people and there's lost people. Yeah. Remember that I told you that. You may never see me again, but sometime down the line you remember you heard it here – that Jesus is Lord. Every knee shall bow!

### Tempe, Arizona November 26, 1979

How many people here are aware that we're living in the end times right now? How many people are aware of that? Anybody wanna know? Anybody interested to know that we're living in the end times? How many people *do* know that? Well, we are. We're living in the end times. That's right. I told you that the times they are a-changing 20 years ago and I don't believe I've ever lied to you. I don't think I ever told you to vote for nobody; never told you to follow nobody... Well, let me tell you now, the devil owns this world – he's called the god of this world. Now we're living in America. I like America, just as everybody else does. I love America, I gotta say that. But America will be judged.

You know, God comes against a country in three ways. First way He comes against them, he comes against their economy. Did you know that? He messes with their economy the first time – you can check it out way back to Babylon, Persia and Egypt. Many of you are college students aren't you? You ask your teachers about this. You see I know they're gonna verify what I say. Every time God comes against a nation, first of all He comes against their economy. If that doesn't work, He comes against their ecology... He did it with Egypt, He did it with Persia, He did it with Babylon, He did it with the whole Middle East. It's a desert now – it used to be flourishing gardens. Alright. If that doesn't work, He just brings up another nation against them. So one of those three things has got to work. Now Jesus Christ is that solid rock. He's supposed to come two times. He came once already; He's coming back again. You gotta be prepared for this...

You just watch your newspapers, you're going to see – maybe two years, maybe three years, five years from now, you just wait and see. Russia will come down and attack in the Middle East. China's got an army of two million people – they're gonna come down in the Middle East. There's gonna be a war called the Battle of Armageddon which is like something you never even dreamed

131

about. And Christ will set up His Kingdom, and He'll rule it from Jerusalem. I know, far out as that might seem this is what the Bible says...

### Omaha, Nebraska – January 25, 1980

Years ago they used to say I was a prophet. I'd say, No – I'm not a prophet. They'd say, Yes – you are a prophet! No – it's not me! They used to convince me I was a prophet. Now I come out and say, Jesus is the answer! They say, Bob Dylan? He's no prophet. They just can't handle that...

### Hartford, Connecticut – May 7, 1980

I don't know if you've seen me before or not. I think I was here sometime in 1964. Anyway, I was singing songs back then. One was a song called "Desolation Row". Huh? You're clapping now, but you weren't clapping then. It was, What's he singing about? They didn't understand what I was singing about. I don't think I did either. Hahahahaha. However, I understand now pretty much what I'm singing about. So it must have taken a while for "Desolation Row", "Maggies Farm", "Subterranean Homesick Blues" and all that stuff to catch on, because it wasn't accepted very well at the time. I've always been prepared for adversity. I was always prepared back then, and now I'm even more prepared...

Walking with Jesus is no easy trip, but it's the only trip. I'm afraid to say I've seen a lot of other kinds of trips. Nobody ever told me Jesus could save me. I never thought I needed to be saved. I thought I was doing just fine. Anyway, now we're living, as you know, in dangerous times. Well, Jesus is prepared for that. He knows all about it... You think what's happening now's bad... you think it's rough now – you just wait! The Bible says, Cursed is the man trusting in Mammon.

### Hartford, Connecticut – May 8, 1980

A long time ago they used to have those Greek plays, pretty long time ago. Anyway, nowadays they got a thing called 'actors'. You know, they're in movies. Back then they had actors too, but they called them 'hypocrites'. That's right. It'd be like a play, y'know, like there'd be a play with about 30 people in it, but actually there'd be only four. They'd all just wear masks; they... *(Dylan pretends to recite in a high-pitched voice)*... to the crowd, talk in another voice, and they'd just wear a mask. So four people could play the parts of 30 people. That's a heavy responsibility. Keeps you on your toes. Never know who you are. So now too there's a lot of hypocrites, talking, using Jesus' name...

Actually, if you wonder why all these things are happening nowadays, Joshua you know, he went into Canaan land, and God told him that in certain times he would destroy all the people – every man, woman, children there. You see, that's bad. Certainly he hated to leave the children, but they was all just defiled. And there was some cities. God said, Don't go in there yet. So Joshua wondered why, and God said, Because their iniquity is not yet full.

So now you look around today. When we started out this tour, we started out in San Francisco. It's kind of a unique town these days. I think it's either one third or two thirds of the population that are homosexuals in San Francisco. I've heard it said. Now I guess they're working up to a hundred per cent. It's a growing place for homosexuals... you know what I'm talking about? Anyway, I would just think, Well, the iniquity's not yet full. And I don't wanna be around when it is!

## Syracuse – May 4, 1980

Some of you might have seen me before and said, What is up with this man? Has he lost his mind? Hahahaha. Well, you know what they say – pop music has always been popular. You know when I was growing up, I used to listen to Hank Williams, Gene Vincent, Little Richard and all those people. I think they formed my style in one way or another. I can't help this type of music I play, this is just the kind of type I've always played...

The devil has taken rock'n'roll music and used it for his own purposes. I know some of you might wonder even if there is a devil. No, I'm not talking about the devil that's got a pitchfork and... are you listening to me? Yeah? Alright. Some of you might have heard about a devil with a pitchfork and horns. That's not necessarily the devil, no. We're talking about that devil – he's a spiritual devil, and he's got to be overcome... We're living in the end times right now, I know we all agree about that. It's the midnight hour. God wants to know who His people are and who His people aren't. Anyway, I saw Bruce Springsteen. I loved him, I really did. Hahaha. Well, you know, Bruce was born to run. Unless he's grabbed or something, he's gonna keep a-running. But you can't run, and you can't hide...

## Pittsburgh – May 15, 1980

They say, Bob, don't preach so much. They always say, Bob, do this; Bob do that. But that's alright. You see, I can do whatever I please anyway, I don't have any friends to lose. I know not too many people are gonna tell you about Jesus. I know Jackson Browne's not gonna do it, 'cos he's running on empty. I know Bruce Springsteen, bless him, is not gonna do it, 'cos he's born to run – and he's still running. And Bob Seger's not gonna do it, 'cos he's running against the wind. Somebody's gotta do it! Somebody's gotta tell you you're free. You're free because Jesus paid for you. That's the only reason you're free. Now, pick up your bed and walk!

## Dayton, Ohio – May 21, 1980

Jesus is for everybody. He came to save the world, not to judge the world. Education's not gonna save you. Law not gonna save you. Medicine's not gonna save you. Don't wait until it's too late now. Lotta people wait until they're old; lotta people wait until they're behind bars; lotta people wait until they're at the end of the line. You don't have to wait that long. Salvation begins right now, today.

# Maria McKee

*At the behest of his then-girlfriend, Carol Childs, Bob Dylan offered a new song, "Go 'Way Little Boy", to the American group Lone Justice. Singer Maria McKee recalls the recording session...*

"...he taught us the song, and he stayed around while we recorded it. He'd brought Ron Wood with him and they played on it, but we ended up working on it a very long time, hanging out 'til like two in the morning in the studio, because he didn't like the way I sang it. It was very frustrating. It got to the point where finally I sang the song *exactly* like him, just did my best Bob Dylan imitation, and he said, 'Ah now you're doing some *real* singing! Now you're doing some *real* singing!'"

*(Interview: Thomas Lasarzik)*

135

# Charlie Quintana

## Interviewed by John Bauldie

*Chalo "Charlie" Quintana, once a Plugz, then a Cruzado, now a Havalina, is one of the best drummers to have played with Bob Dylan. He was interviewed for "The Telegraph" in February 1990, in Paris.*

*The first part of the story is the one I know least about. When did you first meet Bob?*

Well, I got a call. He was doing his first video, for "Sweetheart Like You" off of *Infidels*. I had to do a show the day when I got the call, so I went to the soundcheck for the show, then I ran over to the studio where they were shooting the thing. When I went over I thought I already had the job, but when I got there there were four or five other drummers there, waiting around for the part. I sort of explained to whoever was in charge that I had to split soon because I had to go and play a show, so I was put in first. And I stayed there! They sent the other drummers home and said, OK, you've got to come tomorrow. So I went back the next morning and shot it. I was drum-syncing, however you want to say it, on this extremely simple song...

*Were you given any instructions about what was supposed to be happening in the video – about what the idea of it was?*

No. The thing was just to play. I remember that the night before I could not sleep! I stayed up all night, just from nerves and excitement. I was so hungover the next morning that I put on these little Lennon glasses that I had. I was planning to take them off, but someone said, Oh they look good – leave them on. So I had them on all day long. The band itself was a lot of different people – Greg

Kuehn, who played piano, Carla Olsen from The Textones, Clydie King was singing, a black guy on bass — I don't remember his name... It took 18 to 20 hours to get it done.

*So what happened next?*

From that session for the video, I got word that maybe I could come over to Malibu and jam once in a while. Bob was really cool about it; either he'd call or somebody else would, and they'd say, Come over! Or, Bring another guitar player! So I was picking the people that were going down there. I took a lot of local musicians from Los Angeles: Tony Marsico, bass player for The Cruzados, Jeff Eyrich, who's a producer and a session bass player, Greg Sutton, who ended up playing on the European tour right after that, Steve Hufsteter, the original Cruzados guitar player. Mick Taylor came towards the end...

*Were these just sessions or was Bob beginning to think of putting a touring band together?*

Well, it's hard to know what was really on his mind. My impression of what was going down there is that he was trying to get back into playing, that he just wanted some guys, low-key, to jam. And that's what we did. We didn't sit around and talk a lot. He came in, we played, we had some coffee, we played again. He'd say, Alright, that's it, and he'd split, walk out.

*What sort of stuff were you playing?*

Oh God, listen, we did so much stuff. Every day was different. We did "Maggie's Farm", "Masters Of War"...I remember working on... fuck! What song was this? I mean, it was always like you never knew what was going to come up. There was this one song... What was it? Da da da...da da...I'll remember it in a minute...

*So tell me about the Letterman show.*

The Letterman show, originally it was all very vague. There was talk of going to Hawaii and doing a show there for his label or something, and then it fell through. And then the Letterman show came out of nowhere really. I think it was about a week's notice. But as it turned out, it didn't really matter whether it was a week or a month because we didn't know what we were going to play until about a minute before we went on the air!

*You were already a band as The Plugz then?*

Yeah. Actually, it was The Cruzados already because I remember when I was in The Plugz, we went to New York, spent four months there, and we played Folk City. And we used to all kid around and say, "Home of Bob Dylan!" Little did we know as soon as we got back to Los Angeles, that's when I got the call to do the video and to go up to Bob's house two or three times a week.

You shoulda heard the phone calls I got! Tell him this! I met him once – give him this! And I went, No, no, no, I'm not giving any messages... I wasn't about to blow it by giving him the crap that he gets from everywhere else.

*So how did the three of you end up playing on the Letterman show?*

It was Tony, myself and J.J. – J.J. Huntsecker.

*They called him Justin Justing...*

Well, he changes his last name. He has many, many names. He was in a band called the 88s that I was playing with also on the side. J.J.'s an excellent slide blues traditional roots guitar player. Him and Bob played really good together. Bob liked him 'cos he really knows his stuff. He's very good. And Tony and I played together a few years as a rhythm section. Bob chose us to play on the show. Word just came.

*Did you rehearse for the show?*

Well, we rehearsed at the TV soundcheck and we'd rehearsed the night before, but the night before we went through 50 fucking songs we didn't know! At the soundcheck they sealed off the studio and all the NBC brass was there 'cos it's Bob, and we'd never start "1, 2, 3...", he'd just start strumming and we'd just jump in and follow it, and it would end the same way – he'd just stop playing. There was none of this, "Da-da-da-da, Boom Boom!" to end a song, none of that!

And it was five minutes before we were supposed to go on and I'm asking Bill Graham, saying "Jesus Christ, we're shitting bricks over here! Can you please go in and ask Bob what songs we're gonna do?" And he'd come back and say, "He's not sure yet." And we're going, "Oh shit! We only learned 150 songs!"

*But by the time of the show, you actually knew that he was going to play "Jokerman" and "License To Kill"...*

No! Uh-uh! As a matter of fact, "Don't Start Me Talking" ...I don't even remember going over that before the show!

*So you're on network TV, you're playing live, and Bob opens with a song you never heard before?*

Hey, man, I'm fucking *doing* it, you know? *(Laughs)* You gotta think *quick.* I think it came off alright.

*Do you remember the moment in "Jokerman" when Dylan turns around for his harmonica and can't find it?*

I do, I do! See, that's the thing that was coolest. Maybe if we had rehearsed a song from beginning to end, it would have fallen apart. But because we were used to not knowing what was happening, when he was fumbling around for the harmonica I was just able to keep on tapping it out – a couple of verses, a chorus. It seemed like 10 years! The cameraman got so bored he actually did a close-up of me! Hahahaha! The director must have been screaming, "Guitar player! Bass player! Guitar player! Bass player! Alright... let's try the drummer!" Hahahaha!

*After that, Bob must've started thinking about going on his 1984 European tour... he'd already been playing with Greg Sutton and Mick Taylor...*

Fuck, man. I wish I would've gone on that. I'm not sure why I didn't... but... y'know... c'est la vie... It would be incredibly pompous of me to say I could have done a better job, but.... that's the way things go. It's Bob's band...

*Did you formally audition for the 1984 tour, Charlie?*

I didn't audition, but I remember it was about a week before the tour started, and I was calling two or three times a day, asking whether or not I was going. They'd say, "We're not sure yet. Call back in an hour." This happened for a fucking week. I didn't sleep for a week. I really wanted to do it... The day they left I felt... I was busted up for a month. When he came back though, I saw him again. I was with The Cruzados and we had a deal with EMI, and we did a whole record for them in late '84. I actually asked Bob if he would come and play harmonica on a song. And he said yes. He came to the studio and he played harmonica on a song called "Rising Sun". The same song was later included on the first Cruzados LP for Arista, but the version we recorded for EMI, with Bob on harmonica, was never released. Just after we'd recorded the LP, EMI went through a big change in bureaucracy and our album got canned and forgotten about. For him to come down and play on that song was more than I could ask for. I could hardly ask him to come and do it again.

*Was that the last time you played with Bob?*

No, there was another session after that, a studio session, proper full blown recording studio at Skyline in Topanga Canyon. I took these two guys, one an incredible bass player and an incredible guitar player, both extremely good technically. I said, When we get there and start playing, just follow me. Just follow me. Rule number one – just follow me. I'd already played with Bob for three months, so I knew more or less the way the routine was. But when we got to the session, these guys both wanted to get the gig so desperately bad and they were just so in awe of Bob that they rushed the whole fucking thing. It sounded like shit. I was so embarrassed, so fucking humiliated...

In the middle of it all I took 'em to the bathroom and said, "What the fuck are you guys doing? I told you, watch me!" But it went over their heads. I didn't do one fancy thing with Bob, I just kept time, which is my job. I like it. So unfortunately that turned out to be just a one-day session.

*Can you remember what you were playing then?*

No, I cannot. I was so... bent out of shape! Wait a minute. I remember we did a version of that song... that I *still* cannot fucking remember! The same song as before... da da da da da dump! Da da da da da dump! Daaaa da da da daaa da daah! "Gimme Some Loving"! "Gimme Some Loving"! I remember doing that song with Bob for two days in a fucking row! Over and over, da da da da da dump! "Gimme Some Loving"!

That was pretty much the last time I had any contact with Bob. You know, when I first got into that thing at his house, jamming with him, I never realised what would happen, people asking me a million questions, and I made a decision that I didn't want to say *anything*. I mean, I don't even know the man. I have no right to say anything. I'm a very small, insignificant part of the whole thing, and a lot of the time, people like me who get the privilege of playing with Bob... I mean, I respect myself as a player too, I work hard at what I do. If you think I play good, it's because I worked hard at it, sacrificed a lot of things, my whole childhood. I'm not regretting that, I'm just saying that everyone deserves respect.

# Leonard Cohen

"I loved Dylan's stuff as soon as I heard it. I was living, in a certain sense, in the same kind of universe that he was living in, so that when I heard him, I recognised his genius, but I also recognised a certain brotherhood in the work. And we have since become... acquaintances. I might even say friends. There is some kind of communion between us.

Dylan, to my way of thinking, is the Picasso of song. People came to me when he put out his Christian record and said, This guy's finished – he can't speak to us any more. I thought those were some of the most beautiful gospel songs that have ever entered the whole landscape of gospel music. When you're talking about a man like Dylan, you can never write him off. He's always going to come up with something beautiful."

# The Night Bob Came Round

## by Raymond Foye

Late one night I sat in Allen Ginsberg's East 12th Street apartment with Allen Ginsberg and Harry Smith, the eminent ethnomusicologist and folklorist. We were looking at a new batch of photographic prints delivered that day by Brian Graham, a freelance printer who had been working for the filmmaker and photographer extraordinaire, Robert Frank. I had proposed editing a volume of Allen's photographs for the American publisher Twelvetrees Press, and we had set about making an initial selection.

Allen proudly displayed a recent portrait of Harry. "You know you're a real menace with that camera," Harry whined in his nasal drawl, and then announced that, as it was 11 o'clock, he was going to bed. Allen and I resumed work, though we were interrupted a few minutes later when the telephone rang. It was Bob Dylan. Could he come over and play Allen the tape of his new album? Of course, Allen replied, and repeated the address, instructing Dylan to yell up from the street, as the doorbells were all out of order. About 20 minutes later, Dylan stood in the street, shouting Allen's name, as a yellow taxi sped off into the darkness. Allen opened the window and dropped down the keys tied up in an old sock. Dylan let himself in and walked up four flights to the tenement apartment. *"Is this sock clean?"* he asked in italics.

Dylan carried a six-pack of beer under his arm, and was accompanied by an attractive middle-aged black woman who spoke only with her eyes. He was wearing black jeans and motorcycle boots, black vest and a half-unbuttoned shirt which showed off a pot belly that Allen saw fit to remark upon – a remark that Dylan saw fit to ignore. Fingerless motorcycle gloves, grey in his hair and beard, yellow nicotine-stained fingers with long nails; shabby, unkempt and very edgy, shifting his feet and taking in the apartment. This was the same apartment where 10 years previously

143

he had brought the *Renaldo & Clara* film crew for a pre-road run-through. At that time Dylan was accompanied by a few musicians, and his then-girlfriend Denise Mercedes. Allen had invited some neighbourhood poets – Gerard Malanga and Rene Ricard. The poet Robert Creeley, in town from Bolinas, had spent the evening sitting at the kitchen table drinking Scotch whiskey and chatting with Rene, spurning Allen's too subtle attempts to lure him in the bedroom where Dylan was hoping to meet a poet whose work he held in great esteem. Creeley's ignoring Allen was perhaps due to the fact that Allen never explicitly stated that Dylan was present. Creeley thought that the sounds emanating from the bedroom were Bob Dylan records, and it was not until Dylan was departing that Creeley realised what had been going down, and he laughed at the absurdity of it all.

"So where's the tape?" Allen asked excitedly. Dylan reached in his shirt pocket and took out a cassette in a plastic case. We sat in the living room, Dylan sprawled on a low couch, as Allen cued up the tape. "I was hoping you could give me an idea for a title," Dylan said. "I never had a *problem* with album *titles*. They always just came to me."

The band kicked in with "Tight Connection". Allen leaned forward, trying to catch the words. "I can't understand the words," Allen complained. "What are the words?" he quizzed Dylan. "Ya have ta lissen," Dylan replied with a surly scowl. Allen shook his head. "I *am* listening. I can't get the *words*. Can you repeat them for me?" By now Dylan was obviously perturbed. "I'm sorry but I just can't *hear* them," Allen repeated. So we played the song over again and Dylan began feeding Allen the lyrics, with a particularly pained expression on his face; slightly embarrassed, almost. Next song. Next song. At one point Allen remarked, "Fancy arrangements."

At another point Ginsberg thought he detected a quasi-religious overtone. "Aha!" he said sarcastically, "I see you still have the judgement of Jehovah hanging over our heads!" "You just don't know God," Dylan replied, twice as sarcastic. "Yeah, I never met the guy," Allen said, ending the exchange. Dylan opened his second beer.

Suddenly Harry Smith was yelling from his room off the kitchen: "Turn down that music! Don't you understand I'm trying to sleep!" I have always known Harry to be a quintessentially perverse character, but this went beyond anything I'd ever thought him

144

capable of. Allen didn't turn the music down, but agreed to switch off the set of speakers in the kitchen.

Soon Dylan stopped repeating the lyrics and Allen began to catch the words, occasionally interjecting his admiration for a particularly well-turned phrase. I continued to sit in a state of paralysis, which only heightened when "Dark Eyes" came on, its melody turned inside out, all structure, no surfeit, no embellishment. To hear "Dark Eyes" for the first time – one of the greatest listening experiences one is ever likely to have in life anyway – with Dylan sitting there, averting his glance, shifting his weight nervously, made me aware of just how rare, how painful it is for him to lay his heart bare this way. The tape ended and there was a long silence as we all stared at our feet.

"What were you thinking of calling the album?" Ginsberg asked at last. "*Empire Burlesque*," Dylan said, somewhat emphatically. Allen nodded. "That was the name of a burlesque club I used to go to when I first came to New York, down on Delancey Street," Dylan volunteered, as if to explain away the obvious political content. (How like him, I later thought, only volunteering information when it will mislead.) "Yeah," Allen replied, "I think that's a good title for it." Dylan looked rather surprised, and then slightly pleased at being confirmed in his hunch. Nothing more was said about the matter. I had my eye on the tape and so did Dylan. He guardedly put it back in his pocket.

"So Harry Smith is living with me," Allen proudly announced. Dylan looked genuinely amazed at this fact. "Harry Smith," he repeated the name slowly. "I've always wanted to meet him." "I'll go get him," Allen said, hurrying out of the room. But Harry, having retired, simply refused to get out of bed. So Allen tried to bum some cigarettes and met with equal resistance. When Allen came back and reported that Harry was not getting out of bed, Dylan looked disappointed but impressed.

"Let me show you what I'm working on," Allen said proudly, and we went into the kitchen. Allen handed Dylan a photograph of Kerouac standing in profile on a New York fire escape, railway brakeman's manual in pocket. "*You* took this photo?" Dylan said incredulously. "I've seen this photo for years, I never knew you took this. These are great." Dylan began shuffling through the new prints. "Man, you have to do an album cover for me sometime." "Great!" Allen replied. "What about this one?" pointing to the tape. "Nah, this one's already finished, but the next one," he promised.

(The following year Allen turned up backstage at a gig in Kansas City, where they both happened to be performing. Allen took out his camera and began snapping pictures. "I'll pay you *not* to do that," Dylan pleaded. "But we have an agreement," Allen protested. "I'm supposed to photograph your next album!") Allen explained how we were putting together a book of photographs for a West Coast publisher, who had requested that Allen handwrite descriptive captions.

Suddenly Dylan became enthusiastic. "I got a great idea. Send me a bunch of photos and I'll write the captions. We can do this book together!" Allen looked surprised. "Yeah, sure," he said, a bit thrown off by the suggestion. "Yeah, man, I'll write little stories to these." (A week later Allen called Dylan's office to make the arrangements. "You realise you may never see these photos again?" Dylan's secretary warned. Allen reconsidered, and decided to ask Robert Frank's advice. "Sure, why not?" Frank replied. "It's worth the risk." A few months later Allen called and collected the photos. The package had not been opened.)

Allen then displayed an edition of his poem *White Shroud*, illustrated by Francesco Clemente and hand-printed in India. Dylan looked it over carefully, silently, for a long time, impressed by the illuminated manuscript treatment. "How much does this cost?" he asked. As I had brought the book by, he referred the question to me. "Twenty dollars," I replied. "And how many of them do you make?" "We made a thousand." "How much does the artist get?" Dylan asked – not so much being crass as just wanting to know the practical, business side of the book. (After all, I thought later, I'd hardly expect him to stand there and discuss the aesthetics.) I gave a brief run down on the split.

Allen tried to interest Dylan in teaching songwriting at Naropa Institute in Boulder that summer. Dylan hedged, and walked into Allen's office, just off the kitchen. He looked at the desk. "Is this where you write your poems?" he asked. "No, I write most of my poems in notebooks. I type them up here." Dylan looked at a wall of books. "You still see Burroughs?" he asked. "I'm seeing him in Boulder next week," Allen responded. "Tell him... tell him I've been reading him," Dylan stammered. "And I believe every word he says."

It was about 2.30 in the morning and Dylan said goodnight. Allen walked him out into the hallway and bid him goodnight. The next day I phoned the apartment. Harry Smith answered. I asked why he hadn't got up the previous night and he mumbled some excuse, but he noted how human Dylan's voice had sounded. I thought that was an apt description of the man.

# Eric Clapton

## Interviewed by Roger Gibbons

*Eric Clapton was interviewed especially for "The Telegraph" in Surrey in May 1987.*

*Your recent career and record releases have been incredibly successful, while Bob seems to have been meandering along somewhat haphazardly. What are you doing right and what is Bob doing wrong?*

I think I just apply myself to what I know is contemporary, and I think Bob just sticks to what he thinks is true. And I think I try to bend with the wind whereas he will always try to stay straight to what he thinks is straight and narrow. When it comes down to it he's essentially a folk musician. Basically, his conscience will always make him fight agaInt commercialism. But I think he's great the way he is, and I don't think there's anything wrong with staying true to what you believe is right.

*Your first contact, I believe, was at a recording session in May 1965 with John Mayall. What was that supposed to be for?*

Well, it was just a jam session. He was interested in John Mayall. John had recorded a song called "Life Is Like A Slow Train Going Up A Hill" and that interested Bob. Bob came in, looked for John Mayall. I was just the guitar player on the session. He had a friend called Bobby Neuwirth who was his kind of court jester at the time. Bobby Neuwirth kept coming up to me and saying, You're playing too much blues, man. He needs to be more country! I didn't actually speak to Bob at this time, I just watched him. We played for about two hours. There was a lot of stuff down on tape. Tom Wilson was behind the desk. The next thing I knew, he was gone. I said, What's up with Dylan? They said, He's gone to Madrid. That was the really weird thing about him.

*What sort of things did you record?*

We did a lot of his blues songs which... he was making it up. He was sitting at the piano and we just joined in.

*It was only a few weeks later that "Like A Rolling Stone" was recorded.*

Yeah, that's true isn't it?

*Did you not do that?*

No. He didn't do any of those songs there.

*Did you see any of those concerts?*

No. I didn't. I wasn't interested at all. Actually, at that point I had no particular respect for him. He was just a folk musician and I was a blues musician. We were worlds apart.

*So when did you first get into Bob's music?*

I think I got into Bob himself when I was living in Chelsea. This friend of mine used to keep playing *Blonde On Blonde*. I could hear something there that was really powerful. I realised he was truly making a crossover. It was very difficult for him to actually get into rock'n'roll. It was very powerful. I started recognising that there was something there. I think the earliest time that I would really get into him was when I actually met him for the first time, during the Delaney And Bonnie tour. It was just kind of "our eyes met across the room" and we recognised a kindred soul, you know?

*What – as musicians, really?*

Deeper than that.

*Deeper than that?*

*(In deep voice)* Way deeper than that.

*Were you at the Isle Of Wight?*

Yes I was. He was Hank Williams.

*Yes! I never thought of that.*

That's the way he was. He was fantastic. He changed everything. He used to have a blues voice but he changed voices, and then suddenly he was a country and western singer with a white suit on. He was Hank Williams. It was like *Nashville Skyline*, you know. When he did *Nashville Skyline* he hit something very powerful. I don't think he really realised it was there before. He really changed his attitude musically to a lot of things. I think, you know, it was then he tapped the roots going back to Hank Williams, George Jones, and all those great country singers.

*I thought the crowd reaction at the Isle Of Wight wasn't negative, but it wasn't really positive.*

They couldn't understand it. You had to be a musician to understand it.

*Some time later, Bob gave you "Sign Language", of course.*

Yes. We co-wrote that.

*Really? I was going to ask you about that because your name is not mentioned.*

Well, I put the chords in and he wrote the words to the song. That was when I was making an album called *No Reason To Cry*. He was just hanging out at a place called "Shangri-la" in California – a studio which used to be a school and before then it was a brothel. He was actually living in a tent in the bottom of the garden. He would keep sneaking into the studio to find out what was going on. Trying to catch me there.

*Living in a tent in the bottom of the garden?*

Living in a tent in the bottom of the garden. He would live in a car. He'll do anything ...

*Are you serious about that?*

I'm absolutely serious. He's not your everyday person.

*You did "Knockin' On Heaven's Door" about 1975...*

...just because I thought it was such a great song. I met a fellow in London who did a reggae version of it and I thought, Yeah, I could do that as well! It's a very spiritual song. What it's saying is, you know, "I've had enough. Take me out of here. I can't take any more. Knocking on heaven's door. Let me in!" That's how I came to play dobro on *Desire*, because of the way I played dobro on "Knockin' On Heaven's Door".

*At the* Desire *sessions you actually played on "Romance In Durango" but you're not mentioned on the album cover.*

I was one of a million musicians there. There were 20 musicians in one room. None of them knew what he was going to do next. He'll just start playing something his way and when he starts to play, especially if you're recording, he'll say, This is the way it goes. If you don't get it then that's the end of the song. You've got to be very quick. He had two or three studios full of musicians all waiting for the session, and I got in there and I was just watching his hands because I didn't know what he was going to play. I didn't know the chord sequences or anything. I was just listening to his voice and watching his hands. I realised maybe it was all a waste of time, but it didn't matter. It was really nice just to be in his presence.

*What did you think of Bob as a performer?*

He was dynamite. Very good. Very cynical, but very good.

*Why cynical?*

Because he didn't seem to care whether anyone was listening to him or watching him or anything. He'd turn his back on you just as soon as look at you.

*At The Last Waltz, Bob seemed to me to be the star of that particular concert, even though it was The Band's...*

It's a very difficult thing to sum up. Yes, him and Van Morrison I think stole the show. Bob can walk on the stage tomorrow, anytime, anywhere... There's very few about with that charisma. When they thought about wrapping up Live Aid, actually someone said to me weeks before, Who would you have to close it? I said, There's nobody else. Dylan. That's it.

*Well, most people would have said Springsteen.*

Springsteen goes back five years, six years. You're talking about 20 or 30 years.

*Yes. I'm not disagreeing, but I suppose that most people today would put Springsteen at the top.*

*(Shakes head)* Don't be silly. Springsteen's actually just the rock'n'roll Donovan.

*Although you say "Who else could finish it?", most people were left a bit cold by the actual performance at Live Aid.*

Because he was fucked up. He was actually put upon very badly. He should have gone on by himself. Also, behind a curtain before he was about to play, they were setting up a whole orchestra for "We Are The World". It was very hard for him to go out there. On top of that, Ronnie and Keith showed up at the last minute and said, Can we play with you, Bob? and 'cos he's sweet, he said, Of course you can, and they go on and they fucked it up. To me they fucked it up. And if he'd just gone out there and sung – done "Masters Of War" or whatever, and on his own, he'd have ended the show. He was joined by two people who couldn't actually cope. They were out of it. It was a long day. They were stoned, pissed all day and it was very late in the evening. Lots of pressure on them. It would have been better if he'd done it on his own, just resisted those two characters and just played on his own, and come up with the goods. He came up with the goods anyway.

*You played at a couple of concerts in 1978.*

Yes. Nuremburg and Blackbushe, Brilliant. Blackbushe was great. I remember someone coming up to him with a little piece of paper asking for an autograph. It's a very visual thing, it won't come out on tape. *(Eric gives a demonstration while talking.)* He took this piece of paper and he said, Where's the pen? The guy didn't have one, so he dropped the paper. The way he did it was so poetic. Cold. He can be cold – a cold man, but always with a sense of humour. That is the greatest thing about him, actually – his sense of humour. He's a poet. Basically he's a poet. He does not trust his voice. He doesn't trust his guitar playing. He doesn't think he's good at anything, except writing – and even then he has self-doubts. Have you heard the thing he wrote about Woody Guthrie?

*"Last Thoughts On Woody Guthrie"?*

That to me is the sum of his life's work so far, whatever happens. That is it. That sums it up.

*People always talk about the lyrics, the poetry, but what about the music? People almost write that off as ...*

What about "Lay Lady Lay"? Can anyone cover that? Can Lionel Richie compete with "Say You Say Me"? His ballads are still the finest things. "If you're travelling in the North country fair". I mean, you name me one ballad of his that doesn't strike here *(touches heart)* you know. He really is a great songwriter. *Nashville Skyline* is an important album – also *John Wesley Harding* – very important albums. He was getting away, getting back to his roots. His way of playing anything is totally hybrid. It doesn't make sense musically to the scholar. When he plays the piano, it doesn't make sense except to the listener, except to him. If you're a musician you'd say, Well, what are you doing there? It doesn't make any sense. The same way as he plays the guitar. It's almost as though everything he does you'll have to wait for a year or two until you've got the actual approach to be able to listen to it. At first listening, everything he does is just real hopeless. Then you look back and realise it's exactly right.

*And if you're actually playing behind Bob, does that make it more difficult?*

No. Nonsense. No. It's always in a musical framework, you understand. He just blows. It's the way he sings. It's the same thing really – you stand back a year later and he's done it exactly right.

*You played at Nuremburg...*

We actually stood on stage facing where Hitler used to address the rallies. Heavy deal, very heavy deal. In broad daylight you could see this archway where the Führer would come out and address the crowd. It didn't work out too bad.

*You spent a lot of time with Bob that year.*

Yeah. We made a promise that 15 years from then I would be his lead guitar player. It'll never come about you know, because, I mean, I've got my thing and he's got his.

*What do you think about bootlegs?*

I don't have any issue on this particular one; no particular issue. I can remember one night playing one of the best concerts of my life, looking down in the front row and seeing a guy with a mike, taping. I had the choice of calling someone from security and saying, Look, there's a bootlegger! I thought, That's going to ruin one of the best concerts I've ever done. The record companies would always be against that situation though, 'cos otherwise musicians couldn't make a living. If bootleggers just ruled the world we wouldn't make a living.

*Some of Bob's stuff, 20 years old from the '60s, is great stuff.*

Well, I have some things of my own which I'll never play anyone – which to me are very personal, like that Basement Tape of Bob's. The original version of "I see my light come shining", I have that somewhere in my collection, and which, perhaps, shouldn't be shared with the public. It's a private part of a musician's identity he doesn't want to share. It's very hard to explain... There's some things I've done that I've put on cassette where if I heard them on the radio I would be so fucking furious. I'd think, That's my *private life*, and I didn't *ever* want *anyone* to hear that, no matter how badly they wanted to hear it. After I'm dead and gone it'll all be out, you know, but for the time while I'm alive that's sacred stuff.

*But you and Bob and a few others are getting to the point where you're almost in the public domain. You know what I mean? You're almost in the situation of the old blues players. If you found a new Robert Johnson track, you'd want to hear it, wouldn't you?*

Yeah, but he's dead and gone, isn't he? You know, I wonder how Robert Johnson would have felt if he'd known all those outtakes that he'd done might be heard. He was a guy who would have taken pride in what he was doing. He would have perfected it *(Eric picks up his imaginary guitar and demonstrates while talking)*. Now... tape is rolling... perfect it and get it right. Take one... sorry, didn't get that right. Take two... so take one you don't ever want to hear again. You don't want anyone to hear take one.

*Of course. But I'd still like to hear it.*

*(Laughs)* I *know*! You've been getting me going there.

*Your lyrics are very personal and a lot of Bob's are.*

Yeah. It's what's happening in my heart, really. It's the only thing I can set down to music. Even that is tough going.

*And that applies to Bob as well?*

I think so, yeah.

*But after all this time you've learned the craft of writing a song, surely you could write a song about anything?*

No craft exists without the participation of the craftsman. If the craftsman does not apply himself, then the craft is not there. So if I don't feel like writing a song, there is no craft, no method. You just start from scratch. Every time I pick up a guitar I have to know where the second string is, where the third string is. You may find that hard to believe, but that's the way it is.

*Could you not write a song for West Bromwich Albion, for example, if they got to the Cup Final? If this miracle happened... or if you were penniless, if you needed to make a buck...?*

No.

*Do you think Bob's lyrics are just too deep sometimes for Mr Average in the street?*

Yeah, I expect so. I expect they pass right over Mr Average's head because they speak of the inner soul, of private pain, of the self, personal recognition – a private awakening. Mr Average just wants to be dulled...

*Why did Bob give you the songs in 1978 – "If I Don't Be There By Morning"...*

Well, he just laid this cassette on me with, you know... I was at Nurburgring for the racecourse, just near there. He was hooked up with this girl called Helena Springs. They were co-writing, and I think he was very proud of it and laid it on me... I've still got that on a cassette of them two. Have you got that?

*No, but I'll listen to it later, if you like, Eric.*

That's another bootleg. I've got a private copy of that. When I get down sometimes, I listen to it and it will bring me right out, because I know that no-one else has got it. This was a gift to me. The funny thing was when we next met after Nuremburg was at Blackbushe in fact. By the time of Blackbushe I'd been into the studio and done "If I Don't Be There By Morning" and "Walk Out In The Rain", two or three songs – and in a coach at Blackbushe I played them back to him and he said, Well, when are they going to be finished? *(Laughs)* And I realised he was a master. Still is. Always will be. The man's a master.

*Why did Bob give you those songs?*

Well, I don't know. 'Cos I think he recognised that... that I was actually a good spirit and I could probably do justice to the songs. Even if, probably, in his eyes, I didn't.

*Has he offered you any more?*

He actually offered me a song in 1967. He wrote me a song on a piece of paper, wrote out the words and said, You put the music to it. And I lost them! If you ever see a copy of *461 Ocean Boulevard* or *One In Every Crowd* – one of the two albums – you'll see a picture of a man shoeing a horse, with "Is it rolling, Bob?". The song he wrote was called "Standing Around Shoeing A Horse". I came back and lost his actual... lost his lyrics. Lost 'em in the luggage.

*When did Bob give you the lyrics you lost?*

When I went up to Big Pink, to search Bob out.

*I've not seen this documented.*

Well no. It was a low profile thing.

*What was the place like? The atmosphere?*

Very country, like this, but hilly. Richard Manuel was my drinking buddy. Bob was reticent, leading a home life. Van Morrison also called in.

*Did you play with Bob?*

No. I jammed with The Band though. The Band were the best. They developed an understanding, especially with the Basement Tapes. The Band were not frightened of Bob, not in awe of him.

*Were you surprised by the born-again period?*

No. I always saw Bob as religious. Always a deeply religious, moral, humanitarian type of person. I think the born-again thing was blown out of all proportion. Bob goes through changes. Sometimes he's a heavy drinker, sometimes dry. Sometimes he's into dope, then not. He can disappear with a car-load of Mexicans. No phase is the final one.

*You talked before of cycles, peaks and troughs. What do you think was Bob's trough?*

The motorbike accident, I suppose. That was the worst time. Since The Band he's never really gelled with anybody else. But I spoke to Bob last year and he enjoyed playing with Tom Petty and was really enthusiastic. But he's trying to find a direction. I've been through it. You've got to be true to yourself, but you don't always know your own worth. Your music reflects it. Bob's got doubts sometimes.

*What did you think of* Knocked Out Loaded?

I haven't heard it. Sometimes I don't listen to music for long periods.

*You don't know your name's on the inside cover? There's a list of people for special thanks. It just says "Eric".*

Could be another Eric.

*I don't think so. What about the peak?*

The man could come up with something unbelievable, anytime. I suppose if you get down to the nitty-gritty, *Times They Are A-Changin'* was the heaviest record.

*Bob's been getting a few awards lately, and you've got dozens.*

I like them, for the right things. They're a confidence booster, and remind you that people do care. Bob's human. We all like a pat on the back.

*What about the music press?*

They don't understand him. I read reviews of my last album and I thought, If I had to please these people I would have given up years ago. You've got to do what you believe in, no matter what.

*How did you get involved in Wembley 1984?*

I'd just come back from Paris and I thought I'd check Bob out. I was at the side of the stage and Bob gave me that look. Chrissie Hynde kept bumping into me. The first thing you learn about the stage is how much space you give each other. I'm playing and she backed right into me. I didn't know who she was. I thought she was a chick from the audience. I don't think Dylan knew who she was either. He taught me a song on stage. He turned his back to the audience and he was saying the chords to me – C, A minor. Only a king can do that.

# Ron Wood

## Interviewed by John Bauldie

*Ron Wood, former Face, long-time Rolling Stone, was interviewed in London on November 29, 1988.*

*I'd like to talk to you about talking to Bob Dylan.*

Talking to Bob Dylan is the hardest thing to get going.

*But Bob Dylan once said that you were one of the few people he could talk to. Have you heard that?*

Yeah. He's told me that.

*What do you usually talk to him about? Do you have profound discussions about the meaning of life?*

Yes. We have profound Gemini discussions that usually end up disappearing into oblivion! We talk about the most amazingly silly things. When he's in England we examine the TV programmes, and he'll usually want to watch *Jackanory* or something.

In fact, talking to Bob is always a great pleasure because you never know if he's going to be very exuberant and on a roll; if he's really into something, he'll want to keep talking about it. Like last time I saw him, a few weeks ago in Miami, he was going on about the club I have there, Woody's On The Beach. "Hey man, where can I get one of those?"

*What? A club?*

Yeah. He said, "All I've heard about is Woody's On The Beach. Any other places down there where I can get one?" And I said, "If you play your cards right Bob, you can come in on my club!"

*Would you like him as a business partner?*

Yeah! Why not? But it's hard to get Bob to sit down and actually fix anything. But I've not given up! There still may be hope! I'd love him to be involved in it.

*He could be part of the house band...*

I think he's definitely intrigued enough for him to take me up on my offer for him to play there. Just after a gig, or as an interlude or during the day, any time. In Miami, Bob said – I think quite genuinely – how much he'd love to check it out and play there.

*What was the first thing you talked about when you first met Bob? Can you remember?*

That was when he came up to meet me in 1974 at a Faces party in The Greenhouse; he just came up through all these milling people, and suddenly his face came up to me and said, "I love your album." I went, "Oh! Thanks Bob! I've kind of achieved everything I've wanted to now that you've said that!" In a way I always have Bob in mind when I do things, and for him to say that, considering I'd never met him, I felt really good after that. "Give my love to Keith". That was the only other thing he said.

*When did your paths cross again?*

At Shangri-la studios with Eric Clapton, working on the *No Reason To Cry* album. I was also doing a few odds and sods with Rick Danko, and Ian McLagan and Rob Fraboni were in there. And one night I was up on Sunset in Hollywood and I happened to ring Shangri-la and said, "Anything happening up there tonight?" And they said, "Nothing, other than Bob Dylan's here playing." I went, "What!?" They said, "Yeah. Bob's here. Playing bass. On one of your songs." I said, "Don't let him leave!" And we ended up, me and Jesse Ed Davis and Eric and... I'm not sure of it was Danko or Jamie Oldacre... it must have been Eric's band, I remember Marci Levin, Dick Sims, Carl Radle... anyway, this session went on for a couple of days solid.

That's where I got "Seven Days" from. Bob said to Eric – though I was there too – he said, "You can have this song if you want it." And I took him up on it and Eric didn't.

160

*Did he play it for you?*

Oh yeah. He played it to me and Eric in the studio and we recorded it. There's a copy of that somewhere around. I used to have it, but mine got waylaid a long time ago. Bob played some marvellous songs to us saying, "You can have this one, you can have that one."

*Eric Clapton told "The Telegraph" that Bob was living in a tent at the bottom of the garden at Shangri-la Studios.*

Yeah, he's right! Eric told you that? Yeah. Very vivid in my memory that was. He made that tent up, basically, from the clothes on my bed. He made off with my sheets and pillows and everything. At the sessions we very rarely got the chance to have a break and crash, and I'd often try to crawl back to my room to lie down – "Aw, let me get away for a minute!" – and Eric would say *(whines pathetically)*: "Ronnie . . get up. I *neeeed* you! I need your *heeeelp!*" And I'd say, "Awright Eric. If it was anybody but you . . ." But one night I went to creep off to my room and there was no bedclothes at all, and the window was wide open, and I looked out and I could see this tent in the distance, right in the middle of this big field. And Bob had made off with this girl, but she was in a plaster cast - her leg and her arms in plaster! That was quite funny. It was like *Invasion Of The Zombies* or something to see her coming back across the garden.

*You said Bob was playing bass the night you phoned up. Is he any good on bass?*

He tries his hand! He can play his own songs whether it's guitar, bass or piano. I think he's an incredible organist and piano player.

*How did you come to be at The Last Waltz concert? You seem to suddenly appear for the encore.*

At that time I was really broke, and Neil Young and Sandy Castle, Neil's roadie or something, got me up there to San Francisco. I just went to watch. Course, soon as I got there I ran into Ringo and we were just sitting together enjoying the show, and then Bill Graham dragged us out of our seats and said, "You're going up as well!" We were as surprised as anybody else! Neil Diamond, who's one of my pet hates – in fact none of us could understand what he was doing there anyway – came off stage and Bob's just about to go on, and as he came off Diamond said "You're really going to have to go some to follow me, man, I was so great." And Bob says, "What do you want me to do, go on stage and fall asleep?"

*When did you see him next?*

Well, when I was living in Malibu colony, when Sara left him she came over to me and Chrissie, who I was living with at the time. She brought all the family over too and they filled my whole dining room table. I didn't even know what was going on. They'd split up. To see them all stranded in my house... Anyway, we fed 'em and put 'em up for a while.

Some time after that, when I was living in Mandeville Canyon, Jim Keltner rang me up and said, "I wonder if I could bring somebody over tonight?" I said, "Pleasure." So he brought Bob over. I think Bob trusted him then to help him out. He didn't know where to go. So Jim just brought him over so he'd be able to relax, no pressure. And nine times out of ten there'd be a session going on in my garage. He came over a few times, just to hang out. We would just sit there talking in the back room, and he'd say, "I wish I had a place like this. I love your house."

*He had his house out in Malibu...*

He had that A-frame building that kinda never really took off, at Zuma Beach. It was never finished. I heard that he moved the chimney stack in the kitchen about 40 times before the builders gave up.

*Did you see him at all in the time after his conversion to Christianity?*

Yeah. I went to Santa Monica Civic to see him, as Keith says, in his prophet of profit days. He was alarmingly different, preaching to the audience. And even I was shouting at him, saying, "Come on!! Get on with it!!" I knew he wouldn't stay that outrageously committed. I could tell that he wasn't to be tampered with though. You can't ever change what he's gonna do.

*You played on "Heart Of Mine" in 1981...*

At Clover Sound Studio, Steve Cropper's studio, with Ringo Starr, Jim Keltner... Bob was with Clydie King then. He used to go to her for solace all the time then. She was great with him, but they were like chalk and cheese. Two different people you couldn't hope to meet – her a black, outrageous, hamburger-eating soul-singer, and Bob all quiet and white, nibbling off the side of her hamburger. I always remember him trying to share her hamburger, and she was bossing him around and stuff. He needed it at the time. He sees great firey talent in people, and with Clydie, her voice was fabulous and to hear them build a song with him rattling away on the piano just suggesting a melody line and she'd join in, and so would the other girl singers... there was some tremendous stuff on the boil then. Between takes the stuff he was coming out with was just earth-shattering, but to hear the way he's let producers just take his stuff and bury it has surprised me. "Driftin' Too Far From Shore" is a good example of this, a brilliant, fantastic, really vibrant rock'n'roll track – but when you hear it on the record... When he played the record to me I went, "Bob!!! What's *happened*!!!!? What happened to your *piano*!? What's happened to the *drums*!?"

*And what's his response?*

He'll just say, "Oh well. I hardly knew the guy..." – the producer, you know – "...I didn't want to bother him." And I said, "But that's gone down on your album!" He said, "Well... I didn't really know him." And when we'd go in at Clover or at Delta for a playback, every time he'd have the same attitude. The weak side of him would come out. They'd say, "Hey Bob, we don't need this" and he'd say, "Oh. OK." And they'd make a mix to *their* ears, and he'd just stand outside and let them do it. And I'd be saying, "Hey! You can't let these guys... Look!! They've left off the background vocals!" or "What about the drums!?" But there would be something going on in the back of his head which didn't allow him to interfere. And yet if he'd have gone into the control room with the dominance that he had while we were cutting the stuff, it could have been mind-bending.

*He's also recorded lots of great songs that didn't make it on to his records.*

Have you heard "High On A Mountain Of Love"?

*No.*

I've got this on tape – I've got whole sessions that we did in New York with Joe Blaney, who's now Prince's in-house engineer in Minneapolis – it was from a session with the Al Green band. We did six or seven brand new songs. I've still got them on tape. I'll have to play them for you sometime. I can't remember when it was though . . maybe '83? Oh, I know! When was Bob in Ireland?

*1984*

That's when it was, because he came into the studio completely out of the blue with a walking stick from Ireland for me. He went, "Here y'are Woody, from Ireland!" I've still got that stick. "High On A Mountain Of Love"'s a great song – *(sings)* "Half a million people... high on a mountain, high on a mountain..." It's a very up rock'n'roll song. It's a good version. It was at Intergalactic, the old Hit Factory, in New York in my studio time, with the Al Green band. All these guys from Memphis couldn't understand Bob's chord sequences. Every time he started off a new song, he'd start in a new key, or if we were doing the same song over and over, every time it would be in a different key. Now I can go along with that with Bob, but the band were totally confused, and one by one they left the studio. Only a couple of them stayed. They said "You're OK, Woody, but who's your friend?"

*You'd done a session with Bob for Lone Justice some time before that...*

Yeah. He phoned me up – that's when I realised we were old buddies, 'cos he said, "I need some help Woody, please come and play with me on this session I'm doing for this new band." I said, "I'd love to, Bob." And he said, "What do you want down here? Jack Daniel's or what?" And I said, "Yeah, awright, Jack will be fine." And I remember arriving at the studio and opening the door and he leapt out, and he went "Woody!! I've got it for you!!!" – he goes from somebody who never says a word to somebody who's crazy! – "I've got the Jack Daniel's!! Yeaa-aaah!!!" We had a real tearaway night that night, because as is usual with Bob, it doesn't matter if you've gone to play on someone else's session, you're left with him still recording.

And there was a woman engineer that night and we cut about four more songs of Bob's, and we did a fantastic take of one of these songs, and we went in to hear it and this engineer girl said, "Oh, I didn't like it. I didn't take it." And I was so pissed off. But Bob went, "Oh. So you... didn't record that? That whole thing we just played out there?" "No," she said. And he went, "Oh. OK." And I'm fuming. I said, "Bob, what shall we do? Go out and do it again?" And he said, "No, we've already done it." And I said, "Bob, there's no record of it. Let's do it again." So he said, "Awright, we'll do it one more time."

*Could you go over the story of how you came to play with Bob at Live Aid?*

I was friendly with Gary Shafner, a guy with big grey bags under his eyes who used to take all of Bob's problems on his shoulders. He'd do all his bookings and arrangements and he'd hide Bob, make him disappear and so on. And I used to have a good rapport with Gary, and I said, "What's happening with Bob?" And Gary said, "Well, he's in New York and he doesn't know what to do tonight. Do you think you two could get together?" And I said, "Well I live here, man, get him over to my house." So he calls back and says, "Yeah, Bob wants to come. Is it alright if he brings his son Sam?" I said "Sure." So they turned up in an old station wagon and I was playing Max Miller, the old music hall comedian, and Bob had a laugh and I had to make him a tape up. Anyway I rang Keith and said, "Get on over here, Bob's over here." And Keith said, "Why?" And I said, "Well, if you're not interested, piss off." And I put the phone down.

Later in the evening Bob says, "I'm playing in Philadelphia the day after tomorrow." I didn't even know about Live Aid. He says, "It's a big charity thing." He says, "Bill Graham's got a band for me and I have to go along with it." Then he says, "Do you think that maybe you and me could play together sometime?" I said, "Sure. Let's do the gig on Saturday." He said, "Really?" I said, "Yeah. You don't necessarily have to go along with Bill Graham." And I said, "Keith would love to do it too." So I rang Keith up again and I said, "Get over here because Bob wants us to do Live Aid with him." Keith knew about it, so I said, "We're doing the gig with him on Saturday." He said, "You'd better not be lying, Woody." I said, "No, I'm not lying. Come over here."

So Keith comes round to my house, but the first thing Bob says to Keith is "Are you going to Live Aid or are you going to watch it on TV?" And I've already told Keith that we were doing it! And Keith goes, "You lying bastard!!" and starts as if he's going to strangle me.

I'm shouting "Shut up, man!" and Bob's looking a little confused so he decides to go to the toilet. Keith's shouting "You've been telling me all this shit! Why?" I'm saying, "No! I'm trying to give Bob a bit of support." Keith says, "Oh man, you can never do *anything* right." So I say, "Look, sit there. Stop fuming." So then Bob's just coming out of the toilet so I rush upstairs and say, "Bob, do you want us to do this on Saturday or not?" And he says, "Course I do." And now Keith's coming up the stairs too to leave, and I turn Bob around and say, "Well tell him!" And Bob says, "Hey man, will you play this gig with us?" Keith says, "Course I will." And we had a great time from there on.

*How many different songs did you try out?*

Let's just say that we played everything in Bob's catalogue and everything in the Stones' catalogue in those two days.

*And you recorded it all?*

Yeah. I'd love to know where a lot of those tapes are. I gave a lot of them to Keith and some to Bob as well. Bob started to worry 'cos I was recording most of the time. He said, "What's going to happen to those tapes?" I said, "Here. That's what's going to happen. You keep that one, I'll have this one." Bob says, "No, no I didn't mean . ." I say, "Just for your own peace of mind, you hang on to this." Some of the rehearsal tapes from my basement in New York are incredible. We were playing in there for a couple of days. We were playing in the upstairs dining room just before we left for Philadelphia and it was brilliant. When we got to the stadium he was saying, "I wonder what Bill Graham wants me to do?" We were going, "Do what *you* want to do, Bob!" But he was saying, "Bill might make me do this." Very odd. He wanted to be bossed around again. Even going up the ramps – we'd decided what songs we were going to play and he turns and says, "Hey! maybe I should do 'All I Really Want To Do'!" We were going, "Aargh! Oh my God!" And when we got up there they'd cut all the stage PA off and we were very confused. And they were setting up behind us. We were blowing into the wind. And then he bust a string. And the other guitars had already been packed away by the trusty roadie, so I gave him mine. We came off looking like real idiots. But I'd do it again, for Bob.

*It seemed to me when I was watching it then, and again the other day, that you were alert enough to try and hold the thing together, but that Keith was well out of it, playing something else most of the time.*

Yeah, but him and Bob were in step up here! *(Taps head)* When I see that recording, I'm actually very proud of what Bob did that night. His words were brilliant, the songs were right – Hollis Brown and his starving family, "When The Ship Comes In" was lovely. Considering we couldn't hear what the hell each other was doing, I thought it was alright.

The cover of 'PEOPLE' Weekly, July 29, 1985: Keith Richards, Daryl Hall, John Oats, Ron Wood, Tina Turner, Mick Jagger, Madonna, Bob Dylan.

# Tom Petty & The Heartbreakers

*Tom Petty and The Heartbreakers backed Bob Dylan at Farm Aid in 1985 and on tour in 1986 and 1987. These comments are extracted from various interviews given at the beginning of their collaboration.*

*Tom Petty*: What really sets this apart from what Bob had been doing before is this is a real band rather than just a bunch of session guys put together. He said to me once, "This band is kinda like talking to one guy." We can communicate very quickly – pick up the signals real fast. I don't think the band has ever sounded as good as it is now, which is the exciting thing.

It's an interesting thing to be playing and not know who's going to take a solo. Someone'll start and you just look for your hole. If Bob or I are starting to disintegrate, Mike'll jump in. Sometimes we all play a solo at once, which sounds really interesting!

*Benmont Tench*: Dylan knows a million songs, old delta blues songs and stuff like that. Well, they sound like they may be delta blues songs... One night when we did "Clean Cut Kid", it sounded just like Muddy Waters. He knows more chords than anyone I know.

*Tom Petty*: Musically, Bob's certainly thrown everything at us he can, which is very good for us, because there's not many people around who can really stretch us like that. Not to sound egotistical, but there's so few people you can really learn anything from. Maybe he'll throw out something from the Gershwins, or something with a lot of chords that rock'n'roll players normally wouldn't play. He's a very good musician. He's not to be taken lightly. You don't survive that long if you're not good.

*Mike Campbell*: We've learned you don't have to worry about playing everything exactly right. Sometimes it's better to wing it and hope that the magic happens that way instead of trying to polish it into magic. And that's a good thing to know.

*Stan Lynch*: There's nothing tentative about Dylan on stage. I've seen gigs where the songs have ended in all the wrong places, where it's fallen apart, and it's almost as if, in some perverse way, he gets energy from that chaos.

*Tom Petty*: It's funny but people still attach a lot of mystery to Bob. I mean, Dylan's just a guy like anybody else, except he's a guy who has something to say. And he has a personality that makes it his own. There's not many people that can walk into a room of 20,000, stare at them and get their attention. That's not an easy trick.

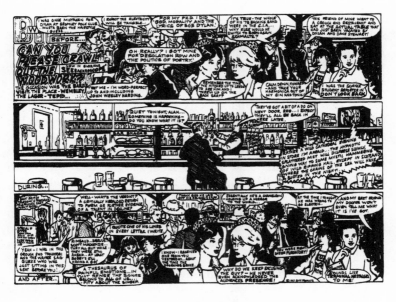

Biff cartoon from *The Guardian* newspaper, 24 October, 1987.

# Hearts of Fire

## Richard Marquand interviewed by John Bauldie

*Richard Marquand, director of* Jagged Edge *and* Return Of The Jedi, *talked to "The Telegraph" in London on June 30, 1987. He had completed* Hearts Of Fire *and was working on a promotional video for the film. A few weeks later he died suddenly, before his Bob Dylan film had been premiered.*

*I'd like to take you back to the beginnings of the* Hearts Of Fire *project, and ask you first of all if you had an idea to do a movie with Bob Dylan, or if the script came along and then you thought of Dylan.*

If you don't mind I'd like to talk even more widely than that, because I think it's important to see the whole of what happened in the context of a person who grew up in the '60s and therefore, necessarily I guess, really felt that he went arm in arm with Bob Dylan as an inspirational source. And so you're dealing with somebody who had always regarded Dylan as being the mainspring of understanding so many social and political events that took place in the '60s, and probably even more importantly in the '70s. I mean I'm one of those people who can remember vividly the first time that he saw Bob, which in fact was on the BBC, on television, as this kid singing "Mr Tambourine Man" and... I'm not saying it changed my life, but what I am saying is that from then on I felt somehow that he was always walking beside me through the rest of the stuff that I did – from then on a series of, to me, very important social documentaries on television about life and the world in the '60s and '70s.

So me, now as a film director setting up a movie and trying to get the script right – I didn't think for one second... it didn't even occur to me that Bob might be interested. It didn't occur to me that Bob even might be reading. It didn't even occur to me that Bob might be still with his feet on our planet. He was, in other words, to me beyond such minor things as Richard Marquand making a movie.

I'd got the script to a point where I was very happy with it. I'd put it through a very very expensive and major re-write, and come up with this very important character Billy Parker who, as you know, represents an older American rock star who retired from the music scene about 10 years ago because he hated the whole business side of the business and preferred just to retire to a farm and make his own friends in his own time, according to his own terms. And when I had the script at that point, I was obviously starting to think that this was a movie that I wanted to make. Before, I wasn't sure. I started to think, Well, who's going to play the part? And I started to meet one or two American contemporary rock stars of the younger generation who might be interested in playing this role, but also in a way people who I was interested in meeting just to find out what it's like in the '80s to be a big American rock star.

And it was at that point that I got a phone call from Bob's agent and friend, who was an old friend of mine, in Los Angeles. She's a very intelligent, very well-educated lady who shared with Bob a great interest in the history of Judaism. And she phoned me up and said, "Richard, had you thought of Bob for the part of Billy Parker?" I said, "No, of course not, how would I possibly? On the other hand, my God! Do you think for one second that it might be possible?" And she said, "Well it's more than possible, he's read the script and he's very interested in talking about it." It was an amazing thing to hear.

Of course subsequently I discovered that he's always been interested in film – I mean not only the Peckinpah film but his own film; that it's always something that has intrigued him, and now at this stage of his life, 46, 47, he's thinking, "Well, let's really try it out, let's see if I'm any good." So that's how initially he and I met. She said, "Well if you're in town," and I was, "and if he's in town," which he was, "why don't I at least set up a meeting and see how you click? I'll take you up to the house and see what happens." So that's what happened.

*Well, you must tell me about the meeting!*

So, I finally got this phone call to say "Meet me at such and such a point in Malibu and I'll be driving a white car and you can follow me up to the house." And I did. And we went up to Point Dume, which is just beyond Malibu – it's a big headland which overlooks a beach, just looks straight out to the ocean. That's the Dylan home which we've seen in photographs and so on and yet suddenly there I am, driving into the open parking lot, with a little funky guard, pillbox, by another gate, which is a chain-link fence. And I go to this guy and he lets us through, 'cos we were expected, and then the chain-link fence swings open and we go through ducks and a duck pond and chickens and down through various bushes, and we park at the house, and go in a hallway that's just lined with newspapers and big canvas sacks. So I go through this hallway in this rather beautiful, very old-fashioned woodsy sort of farmhouse-style ranch house there on the headland, and I go in and there's Bob.

And he's sitting in his kitchen, rather like, I guess, I sit in my kitchen. It's full of today's papers and yesterday's papers and a bottle of wine and wine glasses, piles of letters and cassettes everywhere, and a guitar propped in the corner and somebody washing up in the back. I'm really quite moved to be allowed into his life to that extent, and he is, as I've discovered since, knowing the man, somewhat withdrawn and rather shy, but he's decided I can come in, so I can come in.

And we sit and we spend the rest of the day talking about Billy Parker, the character that he might play, until finally he turned to me and asked, "Well, do you think I can do this?" And I said, "I honestly don't know, what do you think?" And he gave this lovely shy laugh that he has and he said, "Well who's gonna find out? I mean, are we gonna shoot it and find out or what?" And I said, "What we ought to do is get a little video crew together and find some space somewhere – we can either come to your house here or we can borrow a room somewhere – and I'll get Fiona, who was set to play the girl, if the movie went, I'll get her in from New York, and you could have a chance to rehearse the scene with me and work it up a little bit – a couple of scenes – and then, just privately, nobody need know, we'll shoot them on tape. You can look at it, and I can look at it, and if you think you're shit then you can say so, and if I think you're shit I can say so, and we shake hands and, Nice meeting you, Bob."

And that's exactly what we did. And... well, I have to say that I thought that at that point I'd found a movie star. I don't necessarily think that Bob Dylan is gonna play a brain surgeon, or a tank driver, but he's remarkable on the screen. He has enormous internal strength and truth, which is an extraordinary quality to see in a non-actor – screen actor – it's just quite amazing.

*What did you think of his performance in* Pat Garrett & Billy The Kid? *Was that encouraging to you?*

Not really. In fact I made a point the first time we met, in Malibu, to try and find out what happened, because very often, unless you're careful, a director can judge an actor's performance wrongly in another film where they maybe have been bad, and come to the conclusion that that actor is bad. Not that Bob was bad. In fact I thought he was rather interesting in that role, and I think that in a way probably Sam Peckinpah had cast him quite carefully as a sort of icon – he didn't have much of a personality or much to do. On that level I think he worked quite well, and he wasn't called upon to do very much else. And then of course I discovered that what really hurt him was that they took his music and they re-laid it, the studio did, behind Peckinpah's back, so that Bob would write a piece of music for a particular sequence, and then the studio afterwards, in post-production, re-edited the whole thing and put that piece of music against another sequence and just completely screwed up what had been Bob's concept of the movie in conjunction, presumably, with the director who had brought him in to make the movice. And that's disgraceful.

*Yes. It seems that only "Knocking On Heaven's Door" was in the place that he intended it to be.*

Exactly. And "Knocking On Heaven's Door", I imagine, could only be there because it's the story of the song, so it had to go there. Otherwise you can be sure that they'd have moved that to the end as well! Or done something completely dreadful with it!

*Do you remember at the press conference, one of his answers when somebody asked him how impressed he was with you, he said that he was impressed because you drank a lot?*

Oh, did he say that?

*Yes. And there's a story that we've used in "The Telegraph", that Joan Baez once said that if you get drunk with Bob Dylan you can be in his band.*

Well, that's probably true!

*Perhaps it's rather unkind question to ask if alcohol helped in establishing his enthusiasm to work with you!*

Yes! He certainly has a very nice Cabernet Sauvignon there at the house! We certainly managed to get through a few bottles, that's true!

*I thought he was a Jack Daniel's man.*

He certainly is a Jack Daniel's man, yes, but it's not my tipple, boy. I've passed that point in my life now. We got through a little red wine though.

*What had been happening before the filming at Bristol?*

By the time we got to Bristol, we had played some very significant stuff, particularly one important scene between Rupert and him where they first get to know each other and are feeling each other out. It's a really nice scene in which they're sparring, but in a friendly sort of way. So we had shot all the scenes that took place around the Colt mansion in Hertfordshire, which again involved some fairly emotional stuff with Fiona as well, and we'd also shot ... poor Bob, poor Fiona... we'd shot the skinny-dipping scene, which we shot in appalling cold in Black Park Lake, just outside Pinewood. And admittedly Bob didn't have to take his clothes off, but it was his very first dramatised scene.

*There was a gossip column story about Dylan refusing to do the scene because the water was too cold ...*

Oh God it was cold! But he didn't have to go in the water, so that's all made up. Fiona was the brave one because she had to go in — and that was incredible. She took her clothes off and — pish! — in she went.

*Dylan did his bit in cuddly warm water in the studio though, didn't he?*

Yes. Yes. The close-ups were done in the studio.

*Was that done at his insistence?*

No, it was entirely on mine. We could only ever possibly get the wide shots on that night. It was September so how many hours of darkness do you get? We had time for six or seven set-ups of wide shots of Bob, but I knew we'd never... quite honestly you'd never dream of shooting those close-ups of the dialogue, swimming around in water, you wouldn't do them anyway on location. I mean, you'd never get the bloody thing shot.

*There was talk of Dylan's professionalism and keenness on set, but there were other tittle-tattle stories about him having difficulty remembering his lines – in fact remembering a line. Was that something that was true?*

Yes. But the interesting thing about Bob is that I don't actually think that he's got a deceitful bone in his body. I don't think he's ever had to fake anything in his life. He's always sung his own stuff, or stuff of other people that he likes, I mean he's never actually had to fake anything – and therefore in a way he's not glory-bound to be an actor who works all the time, 'cos he can only make this stuff work for him that works for him – he doesn't have any technique. So what would happen that would be quite interesting was that he would stumble on certain lines. And I always used to be very conscious because there always has to be a psychological reason why an actor can remember a whole series of lines and then can't remember a certain line – it's just like psychology really, isn't it? And so I'd pick up on it immediately because otherwise you can waste an awful lot of time, and I'd say, Well, what is it about this? And he would usually be able to figure out that the line had the wrong rhythm or was slightly phony – it's not exactly what Billy Parker would say. It would just be written wrong. And so then we'd change it to make it work for him. And once I'd picked up on that during the shooting, I'd start to spend time ahead of time going through scenes with Bob to make sure that he was comfortable with the dialogue. And if he made changes it was only in step with the intent of the scene – obviously he couldn't re-write the movie to suit himself. It was the original concept, but it was re-written so that he could speak it. That's probably what you heard, and that did happen. Yes. It happened quite a lot.

*Were there any major problems as you were going along? Did things go as well as you'd hoped.*

Well let me tell you, I knew right from the start that Dylan was going to be interesting. And then when we were filming, because Bob is not an actor I realised very quickly that his timing was different from an actor's timing. I mean there's a certain kind of a film timing – we talk in beats, and everybody kind of knows what a beat is – it has a certain rhythm to it. And I've had a tendency in the films I've made to try and break that rhythm – possibly just push it a little bit, speed it up a little bit – I don't know why but I guess it's just my sense of timing. I've been able to manipulate that, and use it in some of the things I've done, so that you can slow things down or perhaps just push them faster at points where you'd expect them to be slower. And I was very interested by the way that Bob worked, and the way that he did things, because his rhythm was never there on the beat. It's probably what surprises people with his live performances and when he records classics that they all know – he never, ever does it the same twice. It's mind-shattering. So when you're watching it, you think, "OK, that's the take I'm gonna use – I'll use a little bit of that take, a little bit of that, but that's the master take." And then you're going through the day, different set-ups and doing different bits and pieces, and at the end of the day you think, "Well I think I've got it. I mean, I think it's really gonna be quite good." And then you go to the cutting room and see this stuff cut together and it's... wonderful! I mean really wonderful... Or I'd watch the rushes and I'd see this close-up of Bob, which after all cinema is about close-ups – it is for me anyway – and I'd see things happening in close-up that I hadn't actually seen watching it live, because the timing was just off. And when I'd expected those things to happen, they hadn't happened – they happened just ahead of it, or just after it.

The man is extraordinary in that way, constantly a surprise. And it's something that Robert De Niro, or in his day Brando, or now Jack Nicholson would give their eye-teeth to achieve in every damn take that they do. It's what they want to do too, but they have to use technique to get there, whereas Bob is doing it out of some kind of natural flow that he has, and it really is quite extraordinary, quite breathtaking.

# Iain Smith

*The producer of* Hearts Of Fire *recalls one of Bob Dylan's lesser-known hobbies...*

"I noticed that he likes to drink whisky a lot. I said to him, You realise I'm Scottish? He said, Yeah, I kind of heard a funny accent. I said, Have you drunk real whisky? None of this American Jim Beam nonsense. He said, I like whisky, it's really great. So I said, Well I'd like you to drink some malt whisky. I told him I was a member of the Scotch Malt Whisky Society, where you can get some very special malts. He said, Oh that sounds good. And I was good to my word, and I arranged for a bottle of a very special malt whisky called Springbank to come down. And I took it into his trailer at Bristol, and he was asleep, So I left this thing at the side of his bed and just went out again quietly. Some time elapsed after that, and then one day he turned around and said, Hey really, I want some more of that stuff you left. It was really amazing. I've never had a whisky like that. It's incredible. Where do I get that stuff? And since then he's become an honorary member of the Scotch Malt Whisky Society, and they're still sending him cases of Springbank."

*(Interview: John Bauldie)*

# Bruce Springsteen

*(Speech on Bob Dylan's induction to the Rock'n'Roll Hall Of Fame, January 20, 1988)*

"The first time that I heard Bob Dylan, I was in the car with my mother and we were listening to, I think, WMCA, and on came that snare shot that sounded like somebody'd kicked open the door to your mind... 'Like A Rolling Stone'. And my mother, she was no stiff with rock'n'roll, she used to like the music, she listened, she sat there for a minute and she looked at me and she said, 'That guy can't sing'. But I knew she was wrong, you know. I sat there and I didn't say nothin', but I knew that I was listening to the toughest voice that I had ever heard. It was lean and it sounded somehow simultaneously young and adult.

And I ran out and bought the single and I ran home and I put it on, the 45, and they must have made a mistake in the factory because a Lenny Welch song came on. The label was wrong. So I ran back, got it, and I came back and I played it. Then I went out and I got *Highway 61* and that was all I played for weeks, looked at the cover with Bob in that satin blue jacket and the Triumph motorcycle shirt.

And when I was a kid, Bob's voice somehow thrilled and scared me; it made me feel kind of irresponsibly innocent, and it still does, when it reached down and touched what little worldliness a 15-year-old kid in high school in New Jersey had in him at the time. Dylan – he was a revolutionary. The way that Elvis freed your body, Bob freed your mind and showed us that just because the music was innately physical did not mean that it was anti-intellect. He had the vision and the talent to make a pop song so that it contained the whole world. He invented a new way a pop singer could sound, broke through the limitations of what a recording artist could achieve, and he changed the face of rock'n'roll for ever and ever.

Without Bob, The Beatles wouldn't have made *Sgt. Pepper*, The Beach Boys wouldn't have made *Pet Sounds*, the Sex Pistols wouldn't have made 'God Save The Queen', U2 wouldn't have done 'Pride In The Name Of Love', Marvin Gaye wouldn't have done 'What's Going On', Grandmaster Flash might not have done 'The Message' and the Count Five would not have done 'Psychotic Reaction'. There would never have been a group named The Electric Prunes. But the fact is that to this day, where great rock music is being made, there is the shadow of Bob Dylan over and over and over, and Bob's own modern work has gone unjustly underappreciated for having to stand in that shadow. If there was a young guy out there writing "Sweetheart Like You", writing the *Empire Burlesque* album, writing "Every Grain Of Sand", they'd be calling him the new Bob Dylan.

That's all the nice things I have to say tonight. Now, about three months ago, I was watching TV and the *Rolling Stone Special* came on and Bob came on and he was in a real cranky mood. He was kind of bitchin' and moanin' about how his fans don't know him and nobody knows him, that they come up to him on the street and treat him like a long lost brother or something. And speaking as a fan, when I was 15 and I heard 'Like A Rolling Stone', I heard a guy like I've never heard before, a guy that had the guts to take on the whole world and make me feel like I had to, too. Maybe some people mistook that voice to be saying somehow that you were going to do the job for them, and as we know as we grow older, there isn't anybody out there that can do that job for anybody else.

So I'm just here tonight to say thanks, to say that I wouldn't be here without you, to say that there isn't a soul in this room who does not owe you their thanks, and to steal a line from one of your songs, whether you like it or not, You was the brother that I never had."

# Bob Dylan & Death

## by Paul Williams

In the autumn of 1980 I visited Dylan backstage at the Warfield Theatre in San Francisco, and at one point he gave me the number of his friend Howard Alk, who he said had really liked my book, *Dylan – What Happened?*, and urged me to get in touch with him. I talked with Howard on the phone, and some months later when I was in southern California, visited him and his wife in Malibu. They were living next door to Dylan's property and, I think, caretaking it for him to a certain extent. They were used to dealing with Dylan pilgrims, joked about our breakfast eggs (from Dylan's chickens) and about the obsessive in each of us.

When I first arrived, Howard's wife told me he was up on the ridge in back of the house, and I went up to meet him. We were sitting on canvas chairs, looking at the ocean, and he said some nice things about my book, but what he really wanted to talk about (I was startled by his seriousness) was the fact that I had overlooked, in his opinion, a major possible factor in Dylan's conversion to Christianity: awareness of and fear of death.

I don't remember much of our conversation – I may have argued that I did call attention to lines like "By this time I'd've thought that I'd be sleeping/In a pine box for all eternity", but if so it was a weak argument, because certainly the text of my book focuses on loneliness, guilt, the search for something to fill the hole left by loss of marriage and family. As soon as Howard spoke, I knew he was right – like any commentator I'd focused on the reasons, the parts of the story that I identified with, and fear of death was not one of them at the time. In hindsight, and in light of comments Dylan has made since, Elvis Presley's death in August 1977 must have had a subtle but very powerful effect on Dylan, particularly in light of Elvis's age and the fact that Dylan in 1977 was 36 and closing fast on the big 40. 40 is mid-life for a lot of us, but for one who identifies himself with other rock stars and culture heroes it can look like the end of the line.

What I didn't know, of course, was that Howard Alk, like all of us, was focusing on the part of the story he identified with. He died, reportedly by his own hand, a year later. I liked him a lot, and am sorry I didn't get to know him better.

Death is a major theme on Dylan's first album, a common obsession of the young, perhaps because leaving home and the loss of childhood confronts us with our own mortality. Thereafter it's a theme that's present throughout his work, as one would expect with any artist, but seldom as a central concern. The *Saved* songs do seem to be about being saved from death ("You have given me life to live") as much or more than from damnation. "Trouble In Mind" and "Slow Train" also refer directly to death as the danger that awakened him. ("She sure was realistic").

The songs about death on Dylan's first album are cover songs, not ones he wrote himself. In 1986, Dylan toured with Tom Petty and The Heartbreakers, and included an unusual number of cover songs in his standard set. Two of the songs he did almost every night are striking in their similarities: "Lonesome Town" ("There's a place where lovers go...") and "Across The Borderline" ("There's a place, so I've been told..."). So what is this lonesome town across the borderline that Dylan is so interested in? What kind of "place" is he singing about? For me, a clear sense of what Dylan is feeling often can be heard in his voice more than his words, and there were moments in the '86 tour when the emotional significance of these two songs came across with particular power. (Tape collectors might want to listen to June 14 and July 17, 1986 to check this out further.)

I need to acknowledge another moment from that extraordinary June 14, 1986 concert in Berkeley before I get to the performances that are most on my mind right now and that forced me to write this article. Dylan sang another cover, "Lucky Old Sun", with real gospel fervour, wonderful relaxed penetrating joy: "...take me to Paradise!/Show me that river, take me across, wash all my troubles away/'Cos that lucky old sun give me nothing to do, but roll around heaven all day". When I heard this in 1986 (and I have to say it sounds even better today – what a fabulous performance) I couldn't help thinking there was something in Dylan (as in all of us, but a little closer to the surface in some) that longed for and looked forward to release from this vale of suffering. ("This time I'm asking for freedom/Freedom from a world which you deny...")

The image is of a physical place, of a body of water to be crossed and a "shore" on the other side and, sometimes, of lost friends waiting on that shore. I wasn't completely surprised to hear Dylan sing "Man Of Constant Sorrow" at the Concord Pavilion on the first night of his 1988 tour, because "Rank Strangers To Me" is the Dylan performance that speaks most powerfully to my heart this year, and every time I hear the lines:

> *They've all moved away, said the voice of a stranger*
> *To that beautiful shore by the bright crystal sea*

I think of "Man Of Constant Sorrow":

> *Your mother says I'm a stranger*
> *My face you'll never see no more*
> *But there's one promise darling*
> *I'll see you on God's golden shore.*

Dylan sang "Man Of Constant Sorrow" twice in his first four 1988 concerts, at Concord and again at Mountain View, June 11. Both performances are exquisite; I'd say Mountain View has the edge, partly because of the spirit with which Dylan leans into the first word of each verse. He garbles a line, and several are unintelligible, but the depth of feeling is so great here, the quality of the singing so amazing, I believe in time this could be regarded as one of Dylan's finer performances. It's a heartbreaker, a real treasure.

An incredible sadness overtook me, a flood of empathy (reminiscent somehow of the mood of the poems in Kerouac's *Mexico City Blues*), the second or third time I heard "Rank Strangers To Me" (recorded 1987?). What an unhappy story this song tells (some kind of a bad dream, "I ain't got no home in this world any more" to the nth level), and how astonishingly penetrating Dylan's vocal performance is here. It just had to be the last song on the album; and I've found myself praying it's not the last song on the last album.

Dylan's 1988 "Man Of Constant Sorrow" is different lyrically from his 1961 recording of the song. He sings six verses instead of four (the last a repeat of the first). The "golden shore" verse is almost unchanged (he sings "friends" instead of "mother", but then it seems likely that the word "mother" and the last verse about going back to Colorado were spontaneous additions during the recording of the first album, related to a fight with his girlfriend's mom). The new verses, which sound like they're traditional (every old ballad has a thousand verses if you do the research) but could have been written by Dylan, contain further references to death:

*You may bury me in some deep valley*
*Where many years I may lay*
*Then you might learn to love another*
*When I am sleeping in my grave.*

And then there's this astonishing, heart-chilling quatrain:

*For six long years I've been in trouble*
*No pleasure here on Earth I've found*
*I'm bound to ride that open highway*
*I have no friend to help me now.*

What are we hearing? Not fear of death, certainly – more like acceptance of it, a welcoming. This does not mean, of course, that our hero is going to leave us soon; but it seems reasonable to guess that the possibility is on his mind. And as always I can only acknowledge him, thank him for sharing his feelings so openly, for letting it all through into his art. I pray as I write this that he survives this tour and keeps going, singing, recording, performing, writing, or just quietly living. But if that's not to be, I guess there's something to be said for dying in the saddle:

*Faretheewell my own true lover*
*I never expect to see again*
*I'm bound to ride that morning railroad*
*Perhaps I'll die on that train.*

1989: "You could never have planned it."

# The Traveling Wilburys

## Interviewed by Roger Scott

*Jeff Lynne:* It was Trembling Wilburys at one point. Me and George were doing George's album, *Cloud Nine*. We had this sort of fictitious group that we might have one day, called The Trembling Wilburys – just like you do in the studio at four o'clock in the morning! Little did we know it would be The Traveling Wilburys.

*George Harrison:* At that point it was just a drunken thought in the back of the head. The way the actual record came about was that I had to do this song because Warners needed a third song to put on a 12-inch single. I didn't have another song, so I just said to Jeff – I was in Los Angeles and he was producing Roy Orbison – we were having dinner one night, and I said, I'm just going to have to write a song tomorrow and just do it. And I said, Where can we get a studio? And he said, Well, maybe Bob, 'cos he's got this little studio in his garage. And it was that instant, you know. We just phoned up Bob and he said, Sure, come on over. Tom Petty had my guitar and I went to pick it up; he said, Oh I was wondering what I was going to do tomorrow! And Roy Orbison said, Give us a call tomorrow if you're going to do anything. I'd love to come along. And that was it!

"HANDLE WITH CARE"

*George Harrison:* When we got to Dylan's house the next morning, we started to write this tune – just the tune. And then, as we were doing that, I thought, Let's just stick a bit in here for Roy. Roy can sing some of it.

*Jeff Lynne:* Yeah, it was great. Just on the lawn in Bob's back garden, all strumming away and saying, Let's get a bit for Roy. And then

Roy tries it out, and it's perfect for him. And it all came together like that.

*George Harrison:* I thought, It's a little bit daft having all these people sat around and then I end up singing it – just get them to sing it! And when they were actually doing the vocals, at one point I just said to Jeff, Hey Jeff! This is it! The Traveling Wilburys! I mean, it was like magic. It just happened – you could never have planned it. If you'd have tried to phone everybody up, you would have got all these record companies and managers and it would have been impossible. But it was so spontaneous, we were doing it before we realised.

*Jeff Lynne:* So this song was delivered for the C-side of a German 12-inch, but when they heard it, they said, Oh, you can't put it on that – it's such a waste of a track. And then we discussed it and George spoke to Roy and Bob and everybody and said, Let's do nine more of the buggers!

*George Harrison:* That's all I could think of, 'cos it was no use to me as a single from *Cloud Nine* – it wasn't on the album, and it was a bit of a throwaway just to use it as a B-side, and the record company were afraid that in America they'd import the track, if it got known, and then start playing it because of the novelty value, and there didn't seem to be any point putting it out like that. But I liked the song and the way it had turned out with all these people on it so much, I just carried it around in my pocket for ages, thinking, Well, what can I do with this thing? And the only thing I could think of was to do another nine – to make an album. And as it happened, they all said yeah – they all loved the idea. It was just a question of timing, 'cos Bob had to go on the road at the end of May, and this is early April when we did "Handle With Care", so he said, Well, I got a bit of time at the beginning of May, so we just said, OK, we'll meet on the seventh of May or something, and we had nine or 10 days that we knew we could get Bob for, and everybody else was relatively free, so we just said, Let's do it! We'll write a tune a day and do it that way. And that's what happened. It was very exciting, and nerve-wracking...

There's a good little story on "Handle With Care", 'cos we got the tune and put it down – all the rhythm guitars just with a little click track, and then we needed the words. And I was walking around with a bit of paper and a pencil, trying to think of a title, and I was saying, Come on! Give us some lyrics then! And there was Bob saying, Well, what's it about? What's it called? And I was looking round in Dylan's garage, and behind the garage door there was this big cardboard box that said "Handle With Care". I said, It's called "Handle With Care", and he said, Oh that's good. I like that! And that was it. Once we'd got the title, it just went off. We could have had 29 verses to that tune.

## "DIRTY WORLD"

*George Harrison:* The second song was "Dirty World". Bob's very funny – I mean, a lot of people take him seriously and yet if you know Dylan and his songs, he's such a joker really. And Jeff just sat down and said, OK, what are we gonna do? And Bob said, Let's do one like Prince! Hahahaha! And he just started banging away – "Love your sexy body! Ooooh-oooh-oooh-oooh bay-bee!" And it just turned into that tune.

*Jeff Lynne:* It was nothing like Prince, really.

*George Harrison:* Nothing like Prince! Nothing like him! But I love that track, it's just so funny. We decided to do this thing about "He loves your... he loves your..." and then we wrote lists. Even that was funny. I don't know how other people write songs, but I just picked up a bunch of magazines and gave everybody a magazine – Roy Orbison had *Vogue*, I had some copies of *Autosport* which I gave to Bob Dylan, and then we just started reading out little things like "five-speed gearbox" and stuff like that, wrote down a big list of things and then we reduced it to about 12 that sounded interesting. And then we just did the take, with the list on the microphone, and whoever sang first, sang the first one on the list, and we sang round the group until we'd done 'em all...

*Jeff Lynne:* ...and every time it came round to Roy Orbison, he always got the "Trembling Wilbury" line. It was the funniest thing, Roy with the operatic voice singing "Trembling Wilbury". We all just collapsed every time. And no matter how we rearranged it, he always ended up with "Trembling Wilbury"! Hahahaha!

## "RATTLED"

*George Harrison:* The album's got to be a bit raggedy because we'd just written the songs and done 'em. We'd write one tune and walk up the garden to the tiny studio – it was more of a control room with a vocal booth, so we didn't have any space to play the guitars. So we set up in a kitchen – it wasn't soundproofed or anything – and we put five chairs around the kitchen, squoze them all in, and put the microphones up and... that's it! So all the acoustic guitar parts were done in the kitchen, and the drummer on "Rattled", he's playing on the refrigerator with these funny little sticks. It had to be a bit rough, but that was the fun of it. We wanted the record to sound good and be like a proper record, but at the same time to have a bit of a rough edge...

## "NOT ALONE ANYMORE"

*Jeff Lynne:* One of the hardest things was to try and make it sound like a Roy Orbison record, because Roy has got the best voice ever in pop music, so it's really tricky to make him fit in...

*George Harrison:* ...and to have a song that's got a good tune to it, 'cos all of Roy's big hits through the '60s, they were great tunes with nice hooks and different little bits... and it was hard to get a song for Roy. Roy was a special case. That song, when we first wrote it, wasn't very good, and Jeff went home and did a bit of homework on it...

*Jeff Lynne:* ...I broke into the studio one morning, came in real early before anybody else got there to try this alternative chord pattern, with the same tune. I put this Telecaster on, playing these other chords, and pulled out all the other stuff. Everyone else arrived and heard it as this new thing and they all loved it. Roy thought it was lovely like that. I just changed the chords.

## "END OF THE LINE"

*Tom Petty:* When we did the video for "End Of The Line" it was very odd not to have Roy there, because we had become a group, and probably still are! Hahaha! Just suddenly, someone's not there. But I think he was there, in a lot of senses, that we could feel him there. It was a little sad, because his funeral was only about a day before the video, but we just tried to go on and hope that we did him justice. And it turned out to be a curious song for the next single, "End Of The Line". It's funny how events come down, and later on, when you hear the song, it can mean so much more than it did when you were writing it. I think the last conversation I had with him was a couple of days before he died, on the phone, and he was just so thrilled that the Wilburys had gone platinum. He was just, "Isn't it great? It's great!"

"CONGRATULATIONS"

*Jeff Lynne:* Bob was the only one who had a clear-cut tune one day, when he came in and said, "What do you think of this one?" It was "Congratulations" and it was almost complete. Those are mostly Bob Dylan's lyrics, but we needed to do sort of like the bridge and a chorus or something...

*George Harrison:* I'm a huge Bob Dylan fan and I've got all his records and I've always liked him and I'll like him and go on liking him regardless of how bad his records are, but I was pleased that he was so into the mood. He really got into it and was comic – even "Congratulations" has got some comical things in there.

"TWEETER AND THE MONKEY MAN"

*George Harrison:* "Tweeter And The Monkey Man" was Bob Dylan and Tom Petty sitting in the kitchen. Jeff and I were there too, but they were talking about all this stuff which didn't make sense to me – Americana kind of stuff. And then we got a tape cassette and put it on and transcribed everything they were saying and wrote it down. And then Bob sort of changed it anyway. That for me was just amazing to watch, 'cos I had very little to do with writing that tune at all, except Jeff and I remembered a little bit that he did that he'd forgotten, which became that chorus part. It was just fantastic watching him do it because he sang.. he had one take warming himself up and then he did it for real on take two, right through. It's just unbelievable seeing how he does it...

*Jeff Lynne:* ...seeing it from the inception, from the first moment he had the idea of going rambling with all these funny "Tweeter And

The Monkey Man" words, to seeing him put the finished vocal on, and producing it as well. It was quite a privilege to watch that.

*George Harrison:* And Bob, from what I've heard, since the Wilburys' record is really writing some fantastic tunes, and his next album he's going to get a producer, and I've no doubt that he'll make a great album. So if that's all the Wilburys did, was help get Bob enthusiastic again, that's something.

# Roy Orbison

## Interviewed by Andy Bell

*London, November 29, 1988*

*Some of the Wilbury songs sound like they were written with you very much in mind.* Not Alone, *for instance, or the bridge in* Handle With Care.

No, not really. I think it's more that people took parts of the songs and made them sound like you'd expect from them. For instance, I tried singing all of "Last Night" but it didn't really work, but the bridge did, so I sang that. The same with "Handle With Care".

*There seems to be a bit of joshing going on in "Tweeter And The Monkey Man". Is there a gentle sideswipe at Bruce Springsteen there?*

Oh no, I don't think so. Bruce is a great mate of mine.

*But all the references to Springsteen songs – "Mansion On The Hill"...*

Well, "Mansion On The Hill", of course, is Hank Williams.

*"Thunder Road"?*

Well, that's Robert Mitchum...hahaha!

*There was always the danger that it might collapse into cliche, wasn't there?*

Sure, there was always the possibility that it would, but that's the thing. It would have been very easy to try to match what we had done in the past, a group of that many talents together trying to write the great rock'n'roll song of the age, and the great ballad, there was a danger of that, but it was really all in fun – not the music, we were serious about that, but we weren't trying to do anything that was great.

*How did your various record companies react when you told them about the album?*

We were working on the Wilburys without any permission from our record companies. If we'd gone to them and said we wanted to do a record together, it would have been very difficult, because you couldn't get CBS and Virgin and MCA and Warner Brothers all to agree on letting their artists do this, so we worked on it in secret, without involving record company attorneys or anything like that. And in the end we just presented it to them. But they were fine about it. I remember one exec said, Well I'm not going to stand in the way of history, and he just hung up the phone. So it was great. They were really gracious about it and there were no problems, no hang ups, not one.

*Had you played with Bob Dylan before?*

I hadn't played with Bob Dylan before. I knew Bob before that for a few years. We weren't really close but I'd been invited to his 25th anniversary party and we talked, and then he came to the studio once to say hello, but we hadn't worked together. Bob was just a prince. I still think of him as the greatest poet of our age.

*I heard that Bob had sent you a demo of "Don't Think Twice" when he was just about unknown...*

I'm not sure that he sent it, but I got the demo of him singing "Don't Think Twice". It was in 1963. I'd just written "In Dreams" and we didn't have any place for it – we only did singles in those days. I didn't record the song. I wish I had've. It was a great song.

*Has he ever sent you any others?*

No, but I always wanted to write with Bob and we got the chance on the Wilburys. And we'll write again. We both live in Malibu and before too long I'm gonna ring him up and go over and we'll do some work, because he's really terrific...

# Daniel Lanois & *Oh Mercy*

## by John Bauldie

*"You need help to make a record, in all the decisions that go into making a record. People expect me to bring in a Bob Dylan song, sing it, and then they record it. Other people don't work that way. There's more feedback."*
(Bob Dylan in *USA Today*)

*"We just played guitar all the time. Everyone was in the same room, and when it started sounding good, we'd record. If I could make all records like that, I would. There were a lot of nice, intimate captured moments."*
(Daniel Lanois in *The Hamilton Spectator*)

Bob Dylan's *Oh Mercy* cannot, it seems, be spoken of or written about without copious reference and deference to its producer, Daniel Lanois, for it was he whose shimmery sound-shaping skills encouraged Dylan to produce what has turned out to be his most celebrated LP since *Blood On The Tracks*. *Oh Mercy* oozes Daniel Lanois, breathes Daniel Lanois – why, it often seems as if it's as much a Daniel Lanois record as a Bob Dylan record. Sometimes it sounds a lot like that too. This is the story of how Lanois came to produce Dylan.

Lanois, Canadian by birth, French by descent, only went to New Orleans, a place he'd never visited before, for a brief vacation in summer 1988, hoping for some Louisiana inspiration for his own LP of Cajun mysticism, *Acadie*. The Neville Brothers heard he was in town, asked him if he fancied "doing a job" on them, and Lanois wound up bringing his "Studio on the Move" ("it's more a state of mind than a specific address") down to record *Yellow Moon*. "The studio fits in road cases," Lanois explained to Mark Cooper, "it's like a big PA and everything's transportable. I usually try and set up

192

one location for a record. With the Nevilles we just set up in their neighbourhood so they wouldn't have to drive very far to come to work. It's a bit like setting up a location for a film – for me it's part of supplying focus."[69]

Lanois rented an apartment in EMLAH Court on St Charles Avenue in New Orleans, and the Nevilles decorated the place with Spanish moss and a couple of alligator heads, before re-christening it Studio In The Swamp. Lanois and Charles Neville lived there, and the band played together in the same room, recording the LP which eventually included versions of "Ballad Of Hollis Brown" and "With God On Our Side". It was, it seems, singer Aaron Neville who wanted to record the Dylan songs. "It was a remark made in passing," Lanois explained. "He hadn't even thought of putting them on the record."[70]

But enter Bob Dylan, whose tour stopped in New Orleans on September 25, 1988. "Bono had heard a few of the songs and suggested that Daniel could really record them right," Dylan explained. "Daniel came to see me when we were playing in New Orleans and we hit it off. He had an understanding of what my music was all about."[71] Dylan subsequently bobbed into Lanois's studio and was pleased with what he found: "You didn't have to walk through secretaries, pinball machines and managers and hangers on in the lobby and parking lots and elevators and arctic temperatures," Dylan observed.[72] Above all, however, he must have been amazed to find Aaron Neville singing "With God On Our Side".

> "He loved it," Lanois said. "He kept going on about it for 20 minutes. He was pretty thrilled to hear it in such a strange setting with that weird backing. He went on and on about it for days..."[73]

It wasn't just the track, but the whole atmosphere that excited Dylan, and he was also impressed that Lanois wasn't just an engineer: "It's very hard to find a producer that can play," Dylan said. "A lot of them can't even engineer. They've just got a big title and know how to spend a lot of money. It was thrilling to run into Daniel because he's a competent musician and he knows how to record with modern facilities. For me, that was lacking in the past."[74] So it was that Dylan came to ask Lanois to be his producer too. So Lanois moved the Studio from EMLAH to the big blue house at 1305 Soniat Street to prepare for the recording of *Oh Mercy*. When Lanois and his gang began to board up the blue house's ground floor windows, anxious neighbours called the police, fearing that the old place was being turned into a crack den. Then, in late March, Bob arrived...

Lanois admits to being a little overawed at the very beginning: "I get stage fright with almost everyone initially, but it goes away as soon as you begin. I was intimidated a little by Bob but he seems very shy and quiet himself."[75]

"Dylan came in with songs completed," said Lanois, "though three were finished off in the studio. For someone to have all their songs ready like he did is very unusual for me. I like it, it's a kind of luxury."[76]

"Yeah, those songs had come to me during that last year," Dylan explained, "and they were pretty much as you hear them on the record. There were some changes but not with the idea of the song picture."[77]

Of Dylan's making changes to the songs in the studio, Lanois further commented, "Dylan's a very committed lyricist. He would walk into the studio and put his head into the pages of words that he had and not let up until it was done. It was quite fascinating to see the transformation that some of the songs made – they would begin as one story and at the end of the night they would be something else."[78]

As producer, Lanois's technique is unusual. In the earliest sessions he just sits in the studio with the musicians, plays, sings, jams, while his engineer, Malcolm Burn, records the entire proceedings on digital audio tape. Then, as the tapes roll, sections which sound as though they might be particularly interesting are marked up to be reviewed at the end of the day. That means that there must be hours and hours of these jamming tapes, eh? "Well, of course. Quite a bit of instrumental work, all of which fell by the wayside. But during this time it was as if Dylan was rediscovering his guitar and there's some nice moments."

Spontaneity, moments of clever invention, guitar-rediscovery – and then? A good deal of hard work.

As well as capturing spontaneous tracks we put in a lot of care with the vocals and the sounds. On the Dylan record there's not really the obvious presence of synthesizers, just straightahead drums and bass and guitars, yet there's this blazing strangeness around it. It's got some wonderful moments, wonderful words, and he's singing great.[79]

The Neville Brothers certainly enjoyed the sessions, as Aaron explained:

> We've known Bob for a while and always admired his songs. Actually playing on his LP was pretty ordinary. His behaviour is shy and introverted. I guess he's someone who has lived under an intense glare of publicity for nearly 30 years, so he's bound to value his privacy, which makes it difficult to get close, but he certainly knows how to achieve that intense chemistry that makes his work so unique.[80]

"With Bob we've recaptured some of the quality that the early records had," Lanois said. "You can really hear him in the foreground and there's a kind of presence, not like a tone control presence but a presence of character and you can't shake it whether you want to or not, it's right there."[81]

"Daniel managed to get my stage voice," Dylan agreed, "something other people working with me never were quite able to achieve."[82]

> It's a blend of his fast approach and my more cautious approach. Quite a few of the things are one take, but care did go into this record. It's not a throwaway, it's got kind of ... if you imagine doing fantastic 70 millimetre filming of simple objects and treating them like jewels, imagine a rugged worker's hand and then closing in on it and examining every pore, every broken fingernail, it's got that kind of quality to it, really in your face. "Ring Them Bells" is just him and his piano and it's a staggering piece of work. His last record had some bad sounds on it and there are no bad sounds on this new record, no cliches. It doesn't take a whole lot to pull the quality out with somebody like Dylan provided he is interested, and he was on this record. You have to show the same kind of interest.[83]

Another song to particularly capture Lanois's interest was "Man In A Long Black Coat":

> It's one of my favourites. It paints a picture of small town Americana, a dance hall on the outskirts of town and how a very strange individual comes in, and 'Not a word of goodbye, not even a note, She's gone with the man in the long black coat...'[84]

It would seem that Lanois's interest and Dylan's sometimes butted up against each other, but only to positive effect:

> "If he came up with songs that you felt weren't up to scratch, would you say so?" Lanois asked rhetorically. "Of course you would, and

that was the case. I did say that I didn't think that certain songs belonged on the record. He took it fine but he bucked me on a few of those decisions. And I would never say no to at least trying out his ideas. We did try a few things that didn't make the finish line. That's the least you can do for an artist, show respect for their own ideas. We had four or six songs that we recorded and didn't use. One track, "Series Of Dreams", was a fantastic turbulent track that I felt should have been on the record, but ... he had the last word."[85]

Lanois, though, was something of a hard taskmaster:

There is a very determined, aggressive side of me. I've been known to kick a chair or two or break a guitar in the absence of commitment. I insist on total commitment. I make that clear and it's made clearer day by day. I give all my energy to the work and a certain respect comes from that. I'm pushing for quality and the artists expect that. When they've run out of energy I have to recognise this and push them, and out of that push will come good work. You can't be kissing too much ass in this job.

With all records there comes a time when people get a little bit lazy, because it's a tiring and unnatural process. At that lull it's very important to take command and turn that lull, turn that valley into a mountain; whatever it takes to reach that mountain is what you have to do at that point to turn the record into a great record. There came a time with Bob Dylan when I felt he fell into old habits – "Get somebody else to play it", he'd say, or "just hire somebody", when really he should have been playing the parts. And I made it clear to him that we weren't going to fly anybody in and we weren't going to have session players play these parts. The parts would be played by the people in the room – by himself, by myself, by the engineer Malcolm Burn, by the neighbourhood guys that we'd chosen to be on the record. It was not going to be a studio record. He was going to play the parts and if they were a little sloppy they would be accepted that way. He understood that at that point...[86]

"Are you good at taking advice and criticism?" Adrian Deevoy asked Dylan.

From someone who has an ear like Daniel Lanois it's more like someone helping you. He's a musician. That helps. My feeling and my hope is that we could work again together because...he made it very painless.[87]

And how did things turn out with Dylan and Lanois outside the studio?

We got on well but we didn't socialise like I'd hang out with the U2 guys. Bob and I shared a couple of interests like motorcycles and pool, but mostly he just went home after work. He's a bit of a home bird these days I think.[88]

# Christopher Parker

## Interviewed by Danny McCue

*Christopher Parker has been Bob Dylan's drummer since 1988. This interview took place during rehearsals for a tour in the USA in the autumn of 1989.*

*How are the rehearsals going for the tour?*

Oh, they're going pretty well. My set-up includes two piccolo snares, one to the left of the hi-hat and sometimes I break one, so we have a spare one on the side, and when Bob came in the other day, we were playing "Queen Jane" or "Just Like Tom Thumb's Blues", doing it kind of march-like, and he picked up this other piccolo snare and started marching around with it. And he really liked the sound, and he said, "We should hook this up so I could play it" and I said, "Sure, no problem." Then we went the next day to get a marching snare drum strap and a marching bass drum harness and hooked it up to the piccolo snare so that he could hold the piccolo snare sideways on his chest and play it. And that's what he's been doing on a couple of tunes, he picks it up and plays it. I don't know if it's gonna be part of the show or what, but it's really funny.

Other than that rehearsals are going pretty good, a lot of new songs and cover tunes. Among the stranger things we did were "I Can See For Miles", the Who tune, "You Keep Me Hangin' On", the Vanilla Fudge version, slow version, "Where Or When" by Rodgers and Hart, "Mystery Train" – that's Junior Parker, something called "12 Volt Waltz", "Sweet Dreams Of You" – Patsy Cline, "Walking After Midnight", "Little Queen Of Spades", I think that's Robert Johnson, "Poison Ivy", "The Blue Ridge Mountains", "High School Hop" – Jerry Lee Lewis, "Mountain Of Love" – Johnny Rivers, "Ring Of Fire", "Give My Love To Rose", "Love's Made A Fool Of You" –

Buddy Holly, "God Only Knows" – The Beach Boys, we do that every set, so that's probably gonna be in there. These are just the cover tunes, but a lot of his new songs too. I'm not sure how new they are, but I never heard 'em before.

I can't pretend to explain his reasons for doing what he does. Sometimes G.E. Smith and I request something, like "Tears Of Rage". I requested "When I Paint My Masterpiece", and he got out the lyric book and sang the lyrics, and to watch him singing, it was like he was rediscovering the songs for himself. It sounded really good. I hope we do it.

*As a drummer, do you think there's a rarely recognised funky swing to Bob Dylan?*

Well that's what I'm always playing with. These tunes, the only thing I have to go on before he starts singing is what he's playing on guitar, and he definitely has his own kind of swing. It's like a shuffle, shuffle the eighth notes, but sometimes the eighth notes are pushed. A lot of times he starts playing something that seems like it's in 12/8, but it's not. He's just shuffled the eighth notes. I like that a lot.

*You're a session drummer. Do you find that when you do sessions, people ask you questions about Dylan?*

Oh yeah, everybody makes jokes – "It's Dylan's drummer!" And everyone does an imitation of him, everybody laughs, I laugh. Certain people flip out and want to know everything – "What's he really like?" Some people have a certain impression in their mind and want that confirmed or denied – "Does he really do this?" And the answers vary – Yes, he does spit on stage. Did he ever hit me? No! Hahaha!

# C'est Commandeur Bob!

## by Dominique Roques

Back in Christmas, 1989, I had a conversation with a friend who happens to be a Director of Music at the French Ministry of Culture. As he was teasing me about my sustained and thus heroic interest in Bob Dylan, I replied with raves about *Oh Mercy* and told him about the forthcoming concerts in Paris. Was Dylan really coming? he asked me. In that case, he suggested, it might be the perfect opportunity for the Ministry to present him with the medal which betokened his award of the prestigious title of Commandeur des Arts et des Lettres, a distinction which had been conferred some six months earlier. I laughed and tried to explain that no, Bob Dylan wouldn't attend. No way. He just didn't do that kind of thing, and nearly 30 years of his public life would prove me right. My friend replied that after what they'd had to go through to get to present the same award to Elizabeth Taylor, anything was possible.

The whole affair slipped out of my mind until Tuesday, January 30, 1990, when I got a telephone call inviting me to be at the Ministère de la Culture on the Rue de Valois for six o'clock that evening. The Salon des Marechaux, in which the ceremony was to take place, is exactly as you might imagine such a place to be – superbly ornate and brightly lit. At the front of a tiny stage microphones had been set up, with TV cameras only a couple of feet away. When I saw them I couldn't believe that the ceremony would happen – I felt sure that Bob would run a mile the minute he saw the way things had been set up. The entire event seemed totally unreal.

While we sipped our warm orange juice in the main room, still incredulous about the entire occasion, Bob Dylan was indeed arriving at the Ministry, and was taken to a private meeting with Jack Lang, the Minster of Culture, who was to confer the honour. Then, at ten past six, a door opened, cameras clicked and flashed, and there, ahead of Jack Lang, was Bob Dylan, walking the 10 yards to the stage with his knees slightly bent and his body and head rocking to a silent rhythm, his hands in front of him, tightly clutching a piece of paper, like a prisoner heading for the scaffold. As the photographers called out to him, his head kept dancing around in a very strange way. Then Jack Lang began to speak:

"I would like to say that for many of us here in France and, of course, in Europe, Bob Dylan represents an ideal of music, life and poetry. And it is therefore a great honour for us all to express our gratitude to him. Tonight, I have the great pleasure, in the name of the Republic of France, to make him Commandeur des Arts et des Lettres."

As the audience applauded, Jack came to the ribbon part of the ceremony, formally awarding the highest honour a foreign artist may receive from France. The new Commandeur unfolded his piece of paper and to a small but indulgent audience, he read out in perfectly intelligible French: "Thank you very much, with all my heart, for the honour that you are doing to me and which touches me deeply. Thank you a thousand times." More applause, more pictures, and then it was over. The private door opened and Dylan was gone.

# Some Bob Dylan Lists

## A: Movies Inside His Head – 16 more lines stolen by Bob Dylan from films...

1        "I don't mind leaving, I'd just like it to be my idea"

*Shane*

2        "You can trust me now"

*To Have And Have Not*

3        "'What's wrong with you?' 'Nothing you can't fix'"

*The Big Sleep*

4        "What would a sweetheart like that Hamilton dame be doing in a dump like this?"

*All Through The Night*

5        "One day you'll be talking in your sleep and when you do I wanna be around"

*I Wake Up Screaming*

6        "I figure we're even. Maybe I'm one up on ya."

*Bend Of The River*

7        "You don't know what love means. To you it's just another four-letter word."

*Cat On A Hot Tin Roof*

8        "'Do you know San Francisco?' 'I've been there to a party once.'"

*Build My Gallows High*

9      "When you live outside the law, you have to eliminate
dishonesty."

*The Line-Up*


10     "What happens here tomorrow is on your head not mine"

*The Big Country*


11     "The love of a lousy buck"

*On The Waterfront*


12     Sulu: "How far do we go along with this charade?"
Kirk: "Until we can think our way out."

*The Squire Of Gothos, an episode of Star Trek.*


13     "It's not a house, dear, it's a home"

*Mr Blandings Builds His Dreamhouse*


14     "No gentleman makes love to a servant in his
mother's house."

*Sabrina*


15     "I've got to move fast – I can't with you around my neck."

*Sirocco*


16     "I don't know whether I'm too good for you or
you're too good for me."

*Sirocco*

## B: 12 songs by other composers that you thought you'd never hear Bob Dylan sing...

1 "Help Me Make It Through The Night" (Kris Kristofferson)
*(Toad's Place, January 12, 1990)*

2 "Dancing In The Dark" (Bruce Springsteen)
*(Toad's Place, January 12, 1990)*

3 "Yesterday" (Lennon/McCartney)
*(Session tape from May 1, 1970)*

4 "Hallelujah" (Leonard Cohen)
*(Montreal, July 8, 1988)*

5 "Boy In The Bubble" (Paul Simon)
*(Grateful Dead rehearsal tape)*

6 "Soon" (George & Ira Gershwin)
*(Gershwin Gala, March 11, 1987)*

7 "I'm In The Mood For Love" (Fields/McHugh)
*(August 3, 1988)*

8 "You Are My Sunshine" (Davis/Mitchell)
*(Johnny Cash session, February 18, 1969)*

9 "And It Stoned Me" (Van Morrison)
*(Rochester, July 6, 1989)*

10 "Da Doo Ron Ron"  (Barry/Greenwich/Spector)
*(Session tape from May 1, 1970)*


11 "All In The Game"  (Sigman/Dawes)
*(October 1981 concerts)*


12 "That Lucky Old Sun"  (Gillespie/Smith)
*(1986 tour)*


## C: A Dozen Records Which Had A Major Influence On Bob Dylan (as listed for *Spin* magazine's Scott Cohen)

1 "Lady's Man"  —  Hank Snow

2 "Lucille"  —  Little Richard

3 "High Lonesome Sound"  —  Roscoe Holcombe

4 "Tom Joad"  —  Woody Guthrie

5 "Mystery Train"  —  Elvis Presley

6 "Not Fade Away"  —  Buddy Holly

7 "Molly And Tenbrooks"  —  Bill Monroe

8 "Get Back"  —  Big Bill Broonzy

9 "Chauffeur Blues"  —  Memphis Minnie

10 "Riding On Train 45"  —  The Delmore Brothers

11 "Ida Red"  —  The Smoky Mountain Boys

12 "Pictures From Life's Other Side"  —  Hank Williams

## D: "Alias anything you please!" – half-a-dozen pseudonyms used by Bob Dylan

1 Robert Milkwood Thomas

2 Blind Boy Grunt

3 Bob Landy

4 Tedham Porterhouse

5 Elston Gunn

6 Elmer Johnson


## E: 10 Great Bob Dylan Songs He's Never Performed In Concert

"As I Went Out One Morning"

"Blind Willie McTell"

"Dear Landlord"

"I'll Keep It With Mine"

"Never Say Goodbye"

"Odds And Ends"

"She's Your Lover Now"

"Sign On The Window"

"Up To Me"

"Went To See The Gypsy"

# F: 10 songs written about Bob Dylan by other people...

### 1 "The Hustler" — Eric Andersen

Dylan's Greenwich Village contemporary expresses his dismay that the erstwhile "choirboy of reality" (ie folk-protest Dylan) seems to have sold out to "the trips, the egg, the golden goose" (ie pop star Dylan).

### 2 "Morgan The Pirate" — Richard Farina

A similarly bitter song by the poet and novelist, grousing about the blue-eyed minstrel: "I appreciate your velvet helping hand, even though you never gave it".

### 3 "To Bobby" — Joan Baez

One-time Queen Of Folk shrilly pleads for former boyfriend to become political again, because "No one could say it like you said it".

### 4 "Song For Bob Dylan" — David Bowie

Melodramatic request for "superbrain" Bob to "walk down the old street" and write songs like he used to: "Give us back our unity...Don't leave us without sanity".

### 5 "Behind That Locked Door" — George Harrison

Former Beatle makes early '70s appeal to his reclusive chum to come on out and play: "The love you are blessed with is worth waiting for/So let out your heart please from behind that locked door".

### 6 "Diamonds And Rust" — Joan Baez

Joan recalls the pleasures and the pain of her ill-starred love affair with "the unwashed phenomenon" whose "eyes were bluer than robins' eggs".

7 "O Brother" — Joan Baez

Outspoken attack on one who "done dirt to lifelong friends with little or no excuses".


8 "Take Me Away" — Roger McGuinn

Memory of boozy days on the road with the Rolling Thunder Revue and "the mystery man all painted like a clown".


9 "Looking Into You" — Jackson Browne

A young, dourly introspective Browne acknowledges Dylan's importance to him as a songwriter: "He opened my eyes to the view/And I was among those who called him a prophet".


10 "At The Warfield" — Greg Copeland

Song about Dylan's first Christian concerts at the Fox-Warfield Theatre in San Francisco, '79: "They tend to put him down but I think the king was back in town at the Warfield," Copeland asserts.

# Notes

1. "My Life In A Stolen Moment" was originally printed in the programme for Dylan's concert at New York Town Hall, April 12, 1963. It has subsequently been reprinted in various collections of Dylan lyrics, most recently in *Lyrics 1962-1985* (Paladin, 1985).

2. Quoted from Robert Shelton's *No Direction Home – The Life & Music Of Bob Dylan* (Penguin, 1987) p66

3. This and most of the other quotations from fellow Sammies are taken from "Brother Bob Dylan: Mr Fraternity Man" by Mark Axelrod, published in the *Minneapolis-St Paul Entertainments Guide* for November 1979.

4. These two extracts of previously unpublished material are taken from 45 pages of Bob Dylan typescripts offered for sale in good faith in spring 1990 by a rare books dealer in Santa Fe, New Mexico called Jean Moss. It is strongly suspected that the papers, mostly written in January and February 1964, were stolen by persons unknown from the home of Albert Grossman, shortly after Grossman's death. The manuscripts were subsequently bought by the singer Graham Nash for $12,000.

5. A tape recording of Bob Dylan singing this song is in circulation amongst collectors of unreleased material. Recorded in May 1961, it is part of a two-tape, 25-song session generally known as "The Minnesota Party Tape" (see Michael Krogsgaard's *Master Of The Tracks – The Bob Dylan Reference Book Of Recording*, SIRR, Denmark, 1988, p16). Until the publication of this interview, it was not known that "Bonnie Why'd You Cut My Hair?" was a Bob Dylan composition, nor that the so-called "Minnesota Hotel Tape" (see Krogsgaard, p22) was recorded in Bonnie Beecher's bedroom.

6. From Anthony Scaduto's *Bob Dylan – An Intimate Biography* (Grosset & Dunlap, 1971) p62.

7. Bob Dylan to Cameron Crowe in the *Biograph* booklet, 1985.

8. Bob Dylan to Jack A. Smith in *National Guardian*, August 22, 1963.

9. As 7

10. From *Baby Let Me Follow You Down* by Eric Von Schmidt & Jim Rooney (Doubleday-Anchor, 1979).

11. Bob Dylan in the Westwood One radio interview with Bert Kleinman and Artie Mogul, July 30, 1984.

12. Bob Dylan in interview with Billy James of Columbia Records for liner notes to the first LP, autumn 1961.

13. Ibid

14. From *Woody Guthrie – A Life* by Joe Klein (Alfred A. Knopf, 1980) p402.

15. Ibid

16. Westwood One, as 11.

17. Ibid

18. Scaduto, as 6, p53.

19. Ibid, p54.

20. Ibid, p60.

21. Arlo Guthrie in uncredited clipping.

22. Scaduto, as 6, p55.

23. Von Schmidt/Rooney, as10, p129.

24. Ibid

25. Scaduto, as 6, p56.

26. Westwood One, as 11.

27. Jeff Steinberg in "Dylan", *Hullaballoo* (US magazine) October 1966.

28. Peter Stampfel quoted in *ZigZag* 26.

29. Joe Klein, as 14, p428.

30. Tom Paxton interviewed by Chuck Hirsch for the now defunct US fanzine, *Zimmerman Blues* (Issue 7, Fall 1977).

31. Nat Hentoff interviewed by Brian Stibal, *Zimmerman Blues* (Issue 6, Summer 1977).

32. Scaduto, as 6, p221.

33. *Time*, May 31, 1963.

34. Robert Shelton, "The Charisma Kid", *Cavalier*, July 1965.

35. Robert Shelton in *Record Mirror*, May 1966.

36. Quoted in *Bob Dylan – The Folk Rock Story* by Sy & Barbara Ribakove (Dell, 1966) p26.

37. Ibid

38. Scaduto, as 6, p89.

39. Ribakoves, as 36, p27.

40. Ibid

41. Shelton, as 34.

42. To Billy James, as 12.

43. Scaduto, as 6, p89.

44. Ibid

45. Ibid, p92.

46. To Pete Oppel, quoted in "Enter The Tambourine Man", *Dallas (Texas) Morning News*, November 22, 1978.

47. To Ron Rosenbaum in "The Playboy Interview: Bob Dylan", *Playboy*, March 1978.

48. Oppel, as 46.

49. Ibid

50. Ibid

51. Ibid

52. To Jonathan Cott in "Bob Dylan: The Rolling Stone Interview, Part Two", *Rolling Stone*, November 16, 1978.

53. To Matt Damsker, *Circus*, September 15, 1978.

54. Cott, as 52.

55. Damsker, as 53.

56. Crowe, as 7.

57. Cott, as 52.

58. Jacket notes to *Biograph*, 1985.

59. Cott, as 52.

60. Crowe, as 7.

61. Damsker, as 53.

62. To Karen Hughes, Dayton, Ohio, May 21, 1980 (published in *The Dominion*, August 2, 1980).

63. To Robert Hilburn, November 19, 1980 (*LA Times*, November 23, 1980)

64. Bob Dylan to the audience, Syracuse Area Landmark Theatre, May 5, 1980.

65. Ken Gulliksen to Dan Wooding, *Buzz*, November 1980.

66. Hughes, as 62.

67. *Buzz*, as 65.

68. Ibid

69. To Mark Cooper in an unpublished interview donated to *The Telegraph*.

70. Ibid

71. To Edna Gundersen in *USA Today*, September 23, 1989.

72. Ibid

73. Cooper, as 69

74. Gundersen, as 71

75. To Liam Fay in *Hot Press*, October 1989.

76. To Gavin Martin in *New Musical Express*, October 7, 1989.

77. Bob Dylan to Adrian Deevoy in *Q Magazine*, December 1989.

78. To Roger Scott on BBC Radio One's "Classic Albums: *The Traveling Wilburys*", broadcast date unknown.

79. Martin, as 76.

80. In *Melody Maker*, October 1989.

81. Cooper, as 69.

82. Deevoy, as 77.

83. Cooper, as 69.

84. Scott, as 78.

85. Cooper, as 69.

86. Ibid

87. Deevoy, as 77.

88. Cooper, as 69.

# The Contributors

**John Bauldie** runs "Wanted Man", the Bob Dylan Information Office, and is the editor of *The Telegraph*.

**Andy Bell** is an investigative reporter for ITV's *World In Action*. He formerly worked for *Time Out* magazine.

**Bert Cartwright**, an American Protestant minister, is the author of *The Bible In The Lyrics Of Bob Dylan*, published by Wanted Man in 1985. Educated at Yale University, Bert has pursued a literary, biographical and artistic interest in Bob Dylan since 1965. His home is in Fort Worth, Texas.

**Chris Cooper** is a 40-year-old charge nurse residing in Peterborough. With Keith Marsh he produced a booklet about Bob Dylan in England in 1965, *The Circus Is In Town*, and he writes monthly in a privately circulated newsletter called *Freewheelin'*. A longer version of his interview with Helena Springs first appeared in the now defunct fanzine, *Endless Road*.

**Raymond Foye** is a publisher and editor who lives and works in New York City.

**Roger Gibbons** is a 39-year-old divorced transport manager who has lived in Woking all his life. His only interests are his children (Terry, Rosie and Laura), music and golf.

**Allen Ginsberg** is one of the most celebrated poets of the 20th century. The material on *Renaldo & Clara*, edited by John Bauldie, was first published in issue 33 of *The Telegraph*.

**Clinton Heylin** is the author of several books, most notably *Stolen Moments*, the Bob Dylan chronology published by Wanted Man. He is currently working on a Dylan biography for Viking Books.

**Danny McCue** is a 28-year-old music journalist residing in Long Island, New York. In the past three years he has contributed to *Spin*, *Newsday*, *Tower Records Pulse*, *Modern Drummer* and *Guitar For*

*The Practising Musician* magazines.

**Miles** co-founded (with John Hopkins) the underground newspaper *International Times* and is the author of several books, including two about Bob Dylan – *Dylan* (Big O, 1978) and *In His Own Words* (Omnibus, 1978). He recently published a biography of Allen Ginsberg (Viking, 1990) and is hoping to begin work shortly on the authorised biography of Paul McCartney. Meanwhile he buys and sells rare books and lives in London.

**Jonathan Morley** writes user guides for computer applications. Despite having originally agreed with Brian Matthew when he said on Juke Box Jury that Dylan was a con-man, almost 25 years (and several thousands of pounds) later he admits to being "somewhere near the top of the third division" of Dylan fans.

**Dominique Roques** is director of a fragrance extraction company in France. He is the author of *Great White Answers* (Southern Live Oak, 1979), a guide to Bob Dylan bootleg records.

**Paul Williams** is the founder of *Crawdaddy!* magazine, editor of *The Philip K. Dick Society Newsletter* and author of 18 books, including *Dylan – What Happened?* (Entwhistle, 1979) and *Performing Artist – The Music Of Bob Dylan* (Underwood Miller, 1990). He attended his first Dylan concert in 1963.

**Markus Wittmann** is a graduate of the University Of California at Berkeley. His interests in history, music and film merged into one project when, in 1988, he began working on a video documentary about Bob Dylan. The project took him across America with stops in Hibbing, Greenwich Village and Malibu, California. The video, entitled *With Truth So Far On*, was completed in May, 1990 and has a running time of three hours.

*If you'd like to subscribe to The Telegraph magazine, send an SAE or International Reply Coupon to Wanted Man, PO Box 22, Romford, Essex, RM1 2RF, UK and you'll be given full information about the publications and the current subscription rates.*

# Index

# Take Back Your Mind

CITADEL UNDERGROUND books are published for people eager to stretch their minds around new and dangerous ideas.

CITADEL UNDERGROUND provides a voice to writers whose ideas and styles veer from convention. The series is dedicated to bringing lost classics back into print and to publishing new works that explore pathbreaking and iconoclastic personal, social, literary, musical, consciousness, political, dramatic and rhetorical styles.

We'd like to stay in touch with you. If you'd like to hear more about our plans for CITADEL UNDERGROUND, please fill out this card and send it to us. We're eager to hear your comments and suggestions.

CITADEL UN**⊕**DERGROUND

*"Challenging Consensus Reality Since 1990"*

Carol Publishing Group • 1-800-447-BOOK
Sales and Distribution Center • 120 Enterprise Avenue • Secaucus, NJ 07094

---

## Please keep me posted about Citadel Underground books!

**Name (Please Print)**_____

**Address**_____

_____

**City**_____ **State**_____ **Zip**_____

**Title of this Book**_____

**Favorite Bookstores (and Locations)**_____

**Fax**_____ **Electronic Mail Address**_____

_____

**Comments**_____

_____

_____

NO POSTAGE
NECESSARY
IF MAILED
IN THE
UNITED STATES

**BUSINESS REPLY MAIL**
FIRST CLASS   PERMIT NO. 111   SECAUCUS, N.J.

POSTAGE WILL BE PAID BY ADDRESSEE

**CAROL PUBLISHING GROUP**

120 ENTERPRISE AVENUE

SECAUCUS, N.J. 07094-9899